THE NEW TESTAMENT AND THE LITERARY IMAGINATION

THE NEW TESTAMENT AND THE LITERARY IMAGINATION

David Jasper

Chaplain and Fellow of Hatfield College, Durham

Foreword by Sallie McFague
Professor of Theology, Vanderbilt University

HUMANITIES PRESS INTERNATIONAL, INC.
Atlantic Highlands, NJ

First published in 1986 in the United States of America by
HUMANITIES PRESS INTERNATIONAL, INC., Atlantic Highlands. NJ 07716

©David Jasper 1987
Foreword © Sallie McFague 1987

Library of Congress Catologing-in-Publication Data

Jasper, David.
The New Testament and the literary imagination.

Bibliography: p.
Includes index.
1. Bible.   N.T.—Language, style.   2. Bible and
literature.   I. Title.
BS2370.J37   1987   225.6'6   86–18519
ISBN 0–391–03482–0

PRINTED IN HONG KONG

For my Mother and Father

'Beyond the desert of criticism, we wish to be called again.'

Paul Ricoeur, *The Symbolism of Evil* (1967)

Contents

Foreword

David Jasper's *The New Testament and the Literary Imagination* falls within a long tradition of British academic writing that is oriented towards educated lay persons. This tradition assumes that intellectual matters are both important to non-specialists and understandable by them. It is an egalitarian tradition that rejects a technical or obscure vocabulary (as well as scholarly footnotes) and insists on a literate prose style. As such, it is a delight to read but must be clearly differentiated from 'popular' writing aimed at those unable or unwilling to deal with difficult questions. Jasper's new book illustrates this tradition admirably: hidden within its deceptively clear mode of expression are several critical, complex current issues of great importance.

I shall refer to only a few, but even these brief remarks will point to the distinctive character of this book – its appreciation for plural interpretations of scripture. Jasper's thesis, expressed in his own words, is that the New Testament texts 'point beyond all the limits which we have set upon them, and our primary response must be to them as language, as structures of words which may indicate to us, without finalising, the meaning of the mysterious event of Jesus Christ'.

I would like to expand on Jasper's appreciation for pluralistic interpretation in regard to two issues. The first issue concerns the search for *one* meaning to a text, a search which, on the American scene, is fuelled by current fundamentalistic and literalistic postures. Because Jasper sees scripture as principally 'mythical literature', as sacred history, whereby a people understands 'the point where history

gives rise to and is invaded by matter of ultimate concern',
scripture is not a collection of historical or doctrinal texts.
Rather, it is an affair of the imagination and as such is not
only open to but actually demands multiple interpretations.
Jasper is appreciative of various critical approaches to the
New Testament, including historical and redactional ones,
but he invites the reader, above all, to approach scripture *as
literature*, to focus on the text as poetic language, for this
way of reading the text allows it to be heard and heard again
– even as the classics are. The New Testament is *kerygma*,
'testimony to the transforming power of the Resurrection',
but the *way* this testimony occurs is through indeterminacy
of meaning and plural possibilities of interpretation, demanding continuous revision and continuous exercise of
judgment. There is no *one* meaning. If scripture is seen as
the work of poets – and Jasper claims this status for the four
evangelists, Paul, and the author of Revelation – the necess-
ity for multiple interpretations is self-evident. Jasper is
certainly not alone in recommending multiple interpretations of scripture or in seeing scripture as poetic. What is
special about his approach is that he takes the reader,
especially the reader with limited tools for engaging in
literary-critical analysis, through a number of exercises in
such criticism. His work is a fine balance between the
theoretical and the practical, between persuading that such
an approach is necessary and showing how it can be done.

A second issue of pluralistic interpretation that Jasper
addresses is that of which genre – story, parable, poetry,
aphorism, and so forth – is most central to the New Testament. Recently in the United States considerable interest
has been directed to 'story' as the premier Christian literary
genre. But as Jasper points out, some people turn to 'story'
or 'narrative' in an attempt to avoid problems in the New
Testament, assuming erroneously that the idea of 'narrative'
is relatively simple. I would add that the current critical
work on narrative by deconstructionists, among others, illustrates Jasper's point concerning the complexity of the form.

Others, Jasper claims, fail to see the great difficulties of moving from 'story' to theology. And finally, the focus on 'story' often obscures the importance of the variety of literary forms in the New Testament. Again, Jasper's sensitivity to pluralism emerges.

I especially appreciated his treatment of the proverb and aphorism in this regard. He mentions Pascal's remark that his own aphoristic form of discourse was the proper way to claim 'true order' in a fallen world, and as Jasper adds, this may be even more true in our time. Such a conclusion seems eminently true to me: in a world threatened by nuclear holocaust, the continuities and comforts of narrative seem unreal to many, whereas the discontinuities and disorientation of aphoristic writing appear more suited to our time of disorder and radical change. If we can believe at all, it is less likely to come about through the seamless web of story with its satisfying beginning, middle and end than through what Jasper calls 'the paradoxical wisdom of the proverbial teaching', which 'reverses the natural expectations of cause and effect, and directs us toward a future hope'. But even here Jasper does not abandon his balanced perspective: aphorism and proverb are to be lifted up *because* they have been neglected due to the hegemony of narrative.

The focus on the text – in its *many forms* – and on multiple interpretations of the text is always at the forefront of his concerns. What informs this perspective is undoubtedly in part his long-term interest in Coleridge which has recently resulted in his book, *Coleridge as Poet and Religious Thinker: Inspiration and Revelation*. Coleridge's view of the human imagination as analogous to the divine act of creation is reflected in Jasper's distinction between fantasy and imaginative literature. The literature of fantasy is escapist, disordered and dreamlike, but the literature of the imagination – Aeschylus, Dante, Shakespeare, and the New Testament – is in some sense *imago dei*. If this is the case, then close attention to the *text as literature* seems imperative. One need not be anxious to get behind the text or to ask to what the text refers, for surely, to interpret the text *as text* is of at least equal importance.

Jasper's appreciation for the text extends, finally, even to its randomness, blurred edges, and contingency. I very much like his refusal to settle for comfortable, smooth readings. The following passage from the book illustrates his sensibility on this point.

> In the New Testament, that confused, baggy monster of a novel, we discover the unutterable particularity of experience, and that the novel being about people (and one person especially) is inevitably random, accidental and liable to break out of formal plans and patterns.

He goes on to comment that, 'St. Mark's Gospel is both funny and tragic, infinitely complex and elusive, like life itself'. Those remarks should be an indication to readers who have been searching for a literary study of Christianity's classic text, which is simple in style but complex in perspective, that they have found one in David Jasper's *The New Testament and the Literary Imagination*.

Vanderbilt University   SALLIE MCFAGUE

Preface

Some time ago I published an article entitled 'On Reading the Scriptures as Literature' in the journal *The History of European Ideas*. It was not an easy paper and, I suspect, its readership was limited and academic. But I dare to believe that what it said was important for a much larger and more disparate group of people who are concerned with the interpretation of the New Testament, including ministers, teachers and students. This book is intended for such people, and indeed for anyone who may read the Bible seriously and critically. I hope that it may give rise to thought without giving offence, for it is offered in a spirit of humility and enquiry.

It is essentially practical, and its origins lie essentially in the practice of preaching and teaching. I have deliberately avoided the methods of historical criticism, although I recognise their value for the study of the New Testament. My hope is to stimulate an imaginative response to these writings, and to provide the reader who has a limited knowledge of New Testament study with means to gain new insights. I am aware that some of my suggestions and arguments may seem almost dangerously removed from the historical foundations of Christian belief. However, I believe that, properly used, the imagination may bring us closer to the secret and mysterious heart of faith and the apostolic witness. Much literary criticism of the New Testament in recent years has tended to generalise from an almost exclusive concern with the nature of parables, narrative and story. The scriptures, however, are a varied and disparate group of writings, representing a wide range of literary genres and written over a considerable period of time. I have given some attention, therefore, to the range of its literature before daring to offer any general comments upon it.

I have not written an academic textbook, and a clutter of references and footnotes can be muddling and unhelpful to readers who want to learn to think for themselves. Therefore, while my debt to certain important authors in this field of literature will be, I suspect, evident, I have restricted my textual references to the Bible itself (using the *New English Bible* translation) and to a very few literary and philosophical authors. More immediately I am indebted to my colleagues and the students in the Department of Theology in the University of Durham for years of debate and discussion. In particular I wish to thank Professor James Dunn for his careful and acute criticisms.

I have included at the end of the book a reading-list of secondary material which I have found particularly illuminating. There are, I am sure, many works which could be included and which I have omitted, but I hope that it may enable those who are interested to continue their exploration of my subject.

Hatfield College DAVID JASPER

ACKNOWLEDGEMENTS

The author and the publishers wish to thank the following who have kindly given permission for the use of the copyright material: Cambridge University Press for permission to use material from the 1970 edition of the *New English Bible*; [*New English Bible* © 1970 by permission of Oxford and Cambridge University Presses]; Michael B. Yeats, Macmillan London and Macmillan Publishing Company, New York, for the use of stanzas III and IV of Yeats's poem 'Sailing to Byzantium' from *The Collected Poems* of W. B. Yeats. Every effort has been made to trace all the copyright-holders, but if any have been inadvertently overlooked the publishers will be pleased to make the necessary arrangement at the first opportunity.

1 Attending to the Text

For the past eight years, in company with countless other preachers and pastors, I have spent much time preparing sermons and talks based upon readings from the New Testament. For part of that time the congregation consisted of the disparate people of a parish in rural Buckinghamshire. More recently my concern has been with a smaller and more limited group of students and staff in the setting of a university chaplaincy. During this later time, preaching has been combined with formal teaching in a department of theology, in which for four years I have endeavoured to conduct courses in the elements of New Testament Greek, the translation and interpretation of St. Mark's Gospel, and literary theory as it bears upon the study of theology.

Such, briefly and plainly, represents the origins of this book. Its form and purpose are simple and straightforward. In short, I wish to offer a number of practical suggestions to those people who may be commencing the study of the New Testament, and to those whose ministry, in school or parish, requires that they continue in that study. I am not a professional New Testament scholar, and do not underestimate the task and achievements of such scholarship. But I suspect that as the academic discipline of biblical interpretation has developed over the past one hundred and fifty years or so, it has tended to adopt certain attitudes and practices which severely limit the reading of the New Testament, not least as it claims to be a testimony to the transforming power of Resurrection. I believe that the skills and insights of the literary critic can effect a certain liberation from such limitations, and I can see no good reason why the study of biblical texts need be restricted to those who are particularly engaged with them as theologians or professional biblical scholars. Nor, indeed, is the literary critic the only other person who may and does give serious attention to the Bible. Philosophers, psychologists, sociologists, anthropologists and countless others have a part to play in a collaborative approach to the sacred texts, which alone, I believe, can recommend them with any degree of adequacy to our contemporary pluralistic society. But, inevitably, my own competence is limited, and must limit the scope of this study.

In chapter 2 I shall isolate three areas of concern in which my own approach to the New Testament finds frequent difficulties when faced with the customary textbooks and commentaries. The first is that of the historical foundation of the gospel narratives and its problematic relationship with the imaginative, 'fictional' manner of so much of the New Testament's reflection upon the life, death and resurrection of Jesus Christ. The second is the tendency of biblical scholars to fragment the books of the Bible, regarding small and sometimes isolated passages without due regard for the continuity of a narrative or the coherence of an artistic whole. The practice in worship of reading and expounding brief extracts in the epistle and gospel, dragged sometimes quite arbitrarily out of context, simply compounds this scholarly tendency. I have already briefly alluded to my third concern, which is that serious readers of the New Testament should be prepared to draw their sense of the text from a critical plurality which recognises the challenge and corrective of a variety of disciplines in the process of interpretation and proclamation.

Above all, my concern is to give proper attention to the text. If that seems oddly naïve, then I suggest that it is precisely something that we are not very good at. Too often we are eager, rather, to use the text as a means of examining the history which underlines it, as a tool for ascertaining the nature of the society which produced it, or as illustrative of the dynamics of the relationships between Jesus and his disciples. Yet again, interpretation so easily misses the point of those infinitely simple and yet profoundly mysterious stories, the parables. The story of the Good Samaritan (Luke 10:30–7), for example, has been poked and prodded across the centuries by interpreters who have seen it as allegory, eschatology, as justifying sending missionaries to Samaria, or as simply weighed down with hidden meanings. And yet the disarmingly simple story remains, its simplicity so manifest that interpreters continually look beyond it for that which only their complex interpretations are capable of disclosing. Sometimes they may perceive something very important (although it frequently has little to do with the parable itself). But often they fail to recognise the obvious truth, that the most profound mystery may lie in the infinitely simple. The real enigma lies not so much in what the parable means as in the nature of what it is about. It is a story about the boundless and indiscriminate nature of neighbourly love, and all other interpretations apart, it sets us pondering upon such unreasonable love. As with any good story, when we begin to read the parable of the Good Samaritan for itself and not for the sake of extraneous doctrinal, cultural or historical considerations, the effect is to direct our gaze through the story itself, to focus upon the truth which is the mainspring of its narrative, the mystery of selfless love. In giving our full attention to the text before us, we realise that the story, like any true witness for Christ, is unself-conscious and self-effacing and that the clearer it is the more clearly we see through the gloss to the greater truth beyond.

In St. Mark's Gospel, Jesus describes his parables as stories told 'to those who are outside . . . so that (as Scripture says) they may look and look, but see nothing; they may hear and hear, but understand nothing' (Mark 4:11–12). Even such disarmingly simple stories mean a great deal more than they seem to say, and conceal mysteries revealed only to a privileged few. And if St. Mark's description of the disciples is anything to go by, even that élite often miss the point. For when it comes to talking about the mystery of the highest good, or God, the gospels rightly make heavy demands upon our imaginations and indulge our passion for story-making and story-telling. Stories cheerfully suffer endless elaboration and updating; they weave intricate patterns of relativity in our world of persons and objects; they encourage self-questioning without crude manipulation; and the endless inventiveness of their language is evidence of a deep and inextinguishable fertility in and beyond the ordinary human soul. Stories forged upon the anvil of the imagination take life far more seriously than do the manipulations of the rational in the human mind.They will always break out afresh, never allowing us to drug ourselves out of awareness, or buy ourselves into oblivion, or interpret our problems away. Stories, the bane of the over-sophisticated, have an infinite capacity for vision and insist that the frustrating limitations of the world will be relieved by an ever-new heroism.

This faculty of the imagination is not bound by dogmatic or conceptual thinking. Indeed, by accepting the exaggerations, the illogicalities and the oddities that we find in the parables, it enables thought to expand and think further. Parables leave us thinking, sometimes forcing us to make the effort to piece the text together. In the words of the philosopher Immanuel Kant in *The Critique of Judgement*, they 'occasion much thought without however any definite concept being capable of being adequate to it'. Thus, the Jesus of St. Matthew's Gospel suggests that 'the kingdom of Heaven is like yeast, which a woman took and mixed with half a hundredweight of flour till it was all leavened' (Matthew 13:33). What does he mean? We must use our imaginations.

That exercise is not actually so very different from the exercise of translating the New Testament from its original language, Greek, into English, and it is just as rigorous. Using your imagination certainly does not, in this instance, mean escaping into the realms of fantasy and the imaginary. For just as the process of translating a text from one lan-

guage to another requires, at the very least, a careful knowledge of vocabulary and the rules of grammar, so we might
say that reading the New Testament requires a careful
appropriation of what is being said to our own situation and
circumstances. We might think of the process of 'translation'
in four stages.

First we must be prepared to take the text as it stands in
our bibles with all its problems and shortcomings, believing
in its integrity. It is not in the rules of game to make up
hypothetical stories in order to overcome literary difficulties. If, therefore, we are persuaded that St. Mark's Gospel
properly concludes at chapter 16, verse 8 ('They said nothing
to anyone, for they were afraid'), then we must assume, in
the absence of other evidence, that Mark intended it to be
so. However tempting it may be to suppose that the
evangelist was arrested in the very act of writing, or died
with his pen in his hand, or that his manuscript was torn and
the original conclusion lost (and all these possibilities have
been seriously suggested), we must assume that he intended
to conclude in this abrupt way, and that its oddity is integral
to the text.

But, having invested our trust in the text, our second
move is to be bold. Our attention requires us to ask questions about what is before us, and leave no stone unturned.
Why is a different word used for 'basket' in the accounts of
the feeding of the five thousand and of the four thousand
(Mark 6:43;8:8)? What is the significance of Jesus changing
the verb for 'love' in his threefold question to Peter (John
21:15–17)? Such questions are not necessarily trivial, but
they arise out of a serious concern to penetrate what the
writing is about.

The third task of translation is to begin to appropriate our
sense of the text to our own experience and sense of
ourselves. Take, for instance, a familiar passage from the
writings of St. Paul:

We know that the law is spiritual; but I am not: I am
unspiritual, the purchased slave of sin. I do not even

acknowledge my own actions as mine, for what I do is not
what I want to do, but what I detest.

(Romans 7:14–15)

Most people, no doubt, would recognise that they are not
the people they would like to be. We none of us match up to
the standards that we set ourselves and from time to time do
or say silly or even bad things. Paul admits to such failings in
himself, but what precisely does he mean by the terms
'spiritual' and 'unspiritual'? What he actually says is that the
law is spiritual (πνευματικός), while he is fleshly (σάρκι-
νός). Here we need to be much more careful in the
appropriation and identification of the text with our own
experience.

Finally, and most difficult of all, translation demands that
we balance the way we have read and appropriated the text
with the text as it is written. It is all too easy to use a biblical
text simply as a kind of proof of an already-established
theological or religious position. We can make a text say
virtually whatever we want it to say, by drawing it out of
context or wilfully abstracting elements from it, in order to
underwrite some doctrine or belief. Thus the New Testament can be used, or abused, in debates about the episcopacy, the ordination of women, the involvement of Christians
in politics, and countless other issues. But if our process of
'translation' is to be properly conducted, then our careful
reading must always be measured against an endless attention to the text, to check that we have not embroidered it,
read things into it, or cut away awkward corners.

Part of the problem in achieving such a balance lies in the
tendency of liturgical practice and criticism to fragment the
books of the New Testament, as I have already suggested.
This is by no means only a modern problem. The Midrash-
ists, the Jewish executors of biblical exegesis, although they
assumed the unity of the text of the Pentateuch, had little
sense of its narrative development. They tended to isolate

small sections as the basis for their elaborate interpretative efforts, and the effect is rather like regarding a Shakespeare play as primarily a sequence of individual scenes with a minimal sense of dramatic cohesion. Modern form criticism works rather differently, but the effect is much the same. Its task is to identify original literary units in the text and trace their development from their beginnings until the final form. At worst, therefore, a text can become simply a mosaic of assorted literary scraps, more or less cobbled together into a recognisable sequence. No book has suffered more from such criticism than St. Mark's Gospel. What it often fails to recognise, however, is that the author of the Gospel was an acute and sensitive artist who was deeply aware of the internal resonances, balances and shape of the overall structure of his book. It is, indeed, almost certain that this writer drew upon a wide variety of sources, and the variations in his style is evidence for this. The beginning of chapter 7, for example, betrays Hebraic origins in its clear *paratactical* style. *Parataxis* is the grammatical term for the placing of clauses one after another, with only minimal structural connection. Accordingly, the text here reads: 'And the Pharisees . . . and certain of the scribes . . . and they saw . . . and all of the Jews. . . .' And so on! It is typical of Hebrew style, but not good Greek. The last four verses of chapter 6, however, which briefly describe Jesus' healing ministry in Gennesaret, are written in a good, careful Greek prose style, full of proper subordinate clauses and grammar. We may, with good reason, suppose that the origins of these two adjacent passages were very different.

This Gospel, then, draws on many sources, and its style is uneven, perhaps rough. Nevertheless, its author was a highly competent literary artist and the reader should be sensitive to both its internal patterning of balance and resonance and its overall coherence, focused on the mysterious and frightening figure of Jesus with his confused, uncomprehending and fearful disciples.

No doubt it will be argued that the techniques of redaction

criticism, too, attempt to view a scriptural writing as a whole, putting together what form criticism has torn apart. To an extent, that is quite true, but there is a profound difference between what began in Germany as *redaktionsgeschichtliche Forschung* (redaction-critical study), and what I am proposing here. Certainly we should be grateful that, in the hands of the redaction critic, an evangelist is recognised not merely as a collector or transmitter of traditional material, but as an author in his own right. (I should add that this critical method is in principle applicable only to the synoptic gospels, the Acts of the Apostles, and just possibly the Epistle of James). But at its heart lies the insight that the gospels must be understood as *kerygma*. Now it is clear, for example, from I Corinthians 1:21 ('God chose to save those who have faith by the folly of the κήρυγμα'), that this signifies not the action of the preacher, but his message. Redaction criticism would read the gospels in the light of a theological or evangelistic programme, in the context of which everything written must find its significance.

My fear is that the result of this will be to sink the literature under the weight of an increasingly arbitrary doctrinal system, and the neater it becomes the less it is able to embrace the mysterious oddities and rhythms of the text. Literature will rapidly become simply the handmaid of dogmatic or even ideological formulae. What, then, happens when something in the text does not fit the pattern? Do we reject it, blame a careless scribe, or just ignore it? I believe that our primary duty is to receive it humbly as an integral element within a whole with which we must struggle. The struggle, perhaps, will yield no neat answers, and yet it may profoundly illuminate the mystery which is, by nature, mysterious. And we, at least, shall have given due attention to the text without exercising upon it the tyranny of our own readership and its predilections.

In no sense, however, am I advocating any individualistic, thoughtless or lazy pluralism of readings. But one of the major problems of redaction criticism is that it can be applied to such a limited number of the literary forms in the New Testament. There is in the whole collection of writings a rich diversity and plurality which one can only attribute to the extraordinary vitality of the gospel of Jesus Christ prompting a wide range or responses in a variety of creative forms. The paradoxes, surprises, non-endings and judgements of this literature ought, it seems to me, to draw into play for the contemporary reader the almost infinite number of tools for critical reflective thought that are now available. If theology claims yet to be the queen of sciences, then among her courtiers should be numbered literary criticism, philosophy, linguistics, psychoanalysis, anthropology and many others. As I shall suggest in some detail in chapter 3, the symbols and images of the New Testament, by their very nature, break barriers and, escaping our attempts at definition, capture in their own luminosity the mystery of event and narrative. It is for us quite legitimate to exercise upon these texts whatever contemporary tools may be to hand, recognising that each will be limited in its use and must be applied with humility and respect. For a balanced reading will desire not to distort the text by exaggeration or critical tyranny, but will wish to take its sense seriously in the context of other descriptions of the human condition with whom it may hold fruitful dialogue, and over which its mystery may hover.

2 The Sense of History

HISTORY RESHAPED

At the beginning of the Acts of the Apostles we find these words:

> In the first part of my work, Theophilus, I wrote of all that Jesus did and taught from the beginning until the day when, after giving instructions through the Holy Spirit to the apostles whom he had chosen, he was taken up to heaven.

> (Acts 1:1–2)

In one sense that statement is simply untrue, for it would be absurd to claim that the book which we know as St. Luke's Gospel contained *all* Jesus' actions and teachings from start to finish. But we know what the writer means. The story he has fashioned in his book is a carefully selected and arranged sequence of events and utterances designed to present a comprehensive image of Jesus and his mission. There were, one may assume, countless 'facts' which will have had little or no bearing upon the story the evangelist was writing. Then, if we pass on to the second part of his work, the Acts of the Apostles, one can argue for a deliberate and fine literary artifice in its close structural parallels with the Gospel. Acts begins with Jesus handing over his mission to the apostles and then leaving them to continue where he left off. The whole movement of the Gospel had been towards Jerusalem, the centre of the Jewish world. Acts begins in

11

Jerusalem, and gradually begins to focus on Rome, the centre of the Gentile world, and there Paul eventually lands. Gospel and Acts form a pair of concentric circles, as the Christian message expands to the heart of Judaism and then to the heart of the entire civilised world.

History, therefore, is being reshaped, or rather, being deciphered, in order to give some coherence to what the philosopher William James called its 'irreducible and stubborn facts'. But in this reshaping, a point is reached where it is difficult to distinguish between fact and fiction. A much earlier philosopher, Aristotle, in his treatise *On the Art of Poetry*, had commented that 'fiction is truer and more philosophical than history'. According to Aristotle, it is only in fiction that we gain an intuition of the infinite in finite terms, straight 'facts' and data being tied to their limited and occasional origins.

If we take this claim seriously, we immediately hold up to question the tradition of criticism which sees its task as the reconstruction of the life of Jesus of Nazareth and particularly the circumstances of his Passion. The implication of this is that the central message of the gospels can be recovered in the quest for the historical Jesus, and that, restored to us in the sharp definition of event and date, he will be found to be a Saviour for our time. But the enterprise of these critics failed, and it is not difficult to see why. For at the simplest level the records of history are tricky guides, and to begin our reconstruction of the life of Jesus from the four gospels will immediately pose major questions about the circumstances of his birth as described by Matthew and Luke, or the dating of the Last Supper – was it a Passover Meal or not? The first three synoptic gospels suggest that it was. The Fourth Gospel is different, for the evidence of John 18:28 suggests that the Supper took place twenty-four hours earlier. Interestingly, the apocryphal Gospel of Peter, which was certainly written before the end of the second century, would agree with this dating.

How, therefore, shall we set out to reconstruct the *facts*?

And there is a further and much more serious criticism to be levelled against this pursuit of the Jesus of History. Both Jesus and the New Testament which testifies to him are of their own time. The man and the literature necessarily conform to conventions and a culture which is not our own. Though not myself a historian, I suspect that our notion of 'history', which is built upon a careful and unprejudiced collation of factual evidence, would have meant little to the writers of the Bible since, as I will suggest in some detail later, they were working within a particular notion of 'sacred history'. Or again, we should be very careful when reading many of the healing miracles of Jesus lest we forget that in their society there was believed to be a much closer relationship between physical affliction and divine punishment than we would now subscribe to. Nor, I imagine, do most of us suppose that a demon with an independent power of speech lurks within a person who is mentally ill. Finally, we would certainly be most unwise to use St. Paul's epistles as a guide for assessing the rights of women. Society now is simply different. Neither Jesus nor Paul can be just recreated and made to work for our time as they worked in first-century Palestine.

There is, of course, a radical alternative to this naïve translation of the New Testament as an historical document. It has been suggested that since the historical evidence for Jesus is ambiguous and inconclusive, then it must be asked whether there is any *necessary* logical connection between the substance of our Christian profession and particular events in history. In other words, is the life and death of Jesus intrinsically essential to the doctrine of redemption, so that its historical details are of vital importance? Why should the life of Jesus fulfil this role as no other life?

My answer to these questions is as ambiguous as the historical evidence itself. Yes, a Christian profession must be patient upon the story of a man whom we believe was human, as we are, and therefore existed. But also no, for the New Testament, which is our concern as our only literary evidence for Jesus, regards him as part of the biblical *story* rather than as part of the biblical account of the past. The necessary connection of this story is not, in the first instance, with the facts of history, but with the Old Testament narratives and particularly the book of Genesis. Jesus, in this story, is linked with the divine, mythological accounts of the creation and the fall, the disobedience of Adam and the results of sin. His role is to obey where the first Adam disobeyed; to restore what was damaged; to die in order to recover life; and so on.

The New Testament, therefore, interprets Jesus by incorporating him into the history of the Old Testament as its fulfilment. But this history is not to be simply equated with modern notions of history. It might better be called sacred history, or more precisely in theology *Heilsgeschichte* (salvation history). This is bound to the national history of Israel in so far as it provides a place for the appearance of Jesus and his church. This history of salvation develops in the virgin birth, the death, resurrection, ascension and return of Christ as the foundation and presupposition of our personal relation to God in Christ. Its own relationship to the evidence of documentable fact is not a simple one, and indeed, like a great work of art, its dynamic and effect is to a great extent generated by its own internal energies. In a sense it means literally just what is says without primary reference to some precisely verifiable fact outside itself. Such sacred history is much more closely related to the art of fiction than we have been used to believe, and much more open to the methods of literary analysis.

HISTORY OR MYTHICAL LITERATURE?

I would prefer to describe the New Testament as mythical literature rather than as history, and I find it extraordinary that, when the obsession with the Bible's historicity continually leads to frustration and bewilderment, the historical

approach does not give way to one more fruitful and faithful
to the text. For, as we shall see in a moment, our text of the
gospels repeatedly demonstrates an energetic dismissal of
anything we might describe as historical evidence. The
problem then remains: what more important concern is
taking its place?

In response to that huge question, we might begin by
considering briefly the first two chapters of St. Matthew's
Gospel, in which the evangelist appears to be writing about
things that happened. How accurate an historian is he?
Before we can suggest an answer, we need to determine his
primary purpose in writing. There seems little doubt that he
is mainly concerned to describe who Jesus is: the descendant
of Abraham and David, the anointed one of the royal line.
He is conceived and named according to the prophecy of
Isaiah. He is rejected by his own people and worshipped by
Gentiles. Prophecy is again fulfilled in the flight to Egypt,
the return to Palestine and the settlement in Nazareth. In
other words, Matthew clearly establishes the claim that
Jesus is the Messaiah, ὁ χριστός (1:16).

I do not suppose for one moment that Matthew would
have understood our modern anxiety to get the facts right,
or our modern distinction between fact and fiction. He was
writing sacred history based upon the Old Testament and his
method was what literary critics call *figural*. By that they
mean that an event or person is prefigured in an earlier
incident or character and in some way fulfils it. This, for
example, the manner of Jesus' birth is prefigured in Isaiah
7:14; the massacre of the innocents is prefigured in Jeremiah
31:15; and the flight to Egypt is prefigured in Hosea 11:1.
But if Matthew changed details in Mark in order to emphasise the fulfilment of Old Testament prophecy, such figural
accretions to the text are not necessarily to be dismissed as
fictive and therefore untrue. In the first place, it may be that
the gospels are not so much concerned to communicate
accurate, factual details of the life of Jesus as to convey
imaginatively (imagination, as I have already suggested,

being an important element in knowledge) the sort of person he was, and indeed, is. Second, figural interpretation was a way of writing history, an attempt to validate the historicity of the gospels through the authority of the Old Testament. No doubt Matthew, in his five prophetic citations in these two chapters, would have regarded the Old Testament as historical evidence; because the prophets said thus, it must have happened in this way. But the appearance of the angel to Joseph, the star of Bethlehem, and the flight to Egypt cannot be taken by us as facts. Such things may have happened, but there is no way of proving it, and it would be a fruitless task anyway. Yet that is not necessarily to suggest that they are therefore, in a strict sense, untrue. The actual historical evidence available to Matthew for the birth narratives may have been extremely skimpy, while his purpose in writing was to establish Jesus in his place in salvation history.

I have described the New Testament as mythical literature. *Myth* has been, particularly of late, a word much used in theological discussion. Yet it is still conventionally understood as practically a synonym for falsehood, suggesting the promotion of unverifiable tales about remote ages. I prefer to understand it much more constructively as something collectively motivated which draws together the great, central values of a culture or a faith. In this sense, the function of myth in the faith of Israel or the early Christian community is to explore the point where history gives rise to and is invaded by matter of ultimate concern. To put it more simply, its function is to explore the relationship and rupture between the finite and the infinite. To put it more philosophically, it initiates speculation where the historical is rent by the ontological. In the New Testament that point finds its problematic focus in Jesus of Nazareth.

If it seems that we have strayed a long way from the text of the New Testament, nevertheless these rather delicate suggestions rest upon a sense of the text as literature which is still rooted in history and a way of life which we can recognise and, to some extent, share. But no literature merely transcribes life. Its art does not reduplicate an outer world nor even mirror the facts of history. The tendency, rather, is to concentrate and intensify life, while selecting and shaping history, so that it may exaggerate and distort even in its pursuit of truth. And there is a difference between responsible, imaginative literature, and that which is irresponsible and leads us into the realms of fantasy. Furthermore, the literary art of the New Testament which seeks to represent Jesus Christ for us is a fundamentally theological exercise, for neither is theology a mirror. Like all good imaginative writing it represents a world, but the connection is not literal. In order to remain true to its enterprise, theology substitutes and represses elements in the world it represents, and, as I shall describe in chapter 3, it is essentially *metaphorical*.

Consider for a moment Peter's Pentecost sermon in Acts 2.

Men of Israel, listen to me: I speak of Jesus of Nazareth, a man singled out by God and made known to you through miracles, portents, and signs, which God worked among you through him, as you well know. When he had been given up to you, by the deliberate will and plan of God, you used heathen men to crucify and kill him. But God raised him to life, setting him free from the pangs of death, because it could not be that death should keep him in its grip.

(Acts 2:22–4)

By any standards that is an odd way to present a brief biography, and its oddity stems largely from its description of the life and death of a man in terms of the activity and purposes of God. We shall need to return to that key word for religious language in more detail later. Suffice it here to say that in many ways 'God' is a word which lies outside the ordinary categories of language, and that when a narrative which claims some basis in history begins to employ God-talk as part of its rationale and motivation, it is likely to bristle with improprieties.

THE NARRATION OF HISTORY

In the first place, as we read Peter's sermon, we should not confuse an historical individual (Jesus) with his narrative representation. To regard it as primarily a judgement upon the Jesus of History is to miss the point entirely. The life of a man is described as driven by God. What matters, in the end, is that human life is viewed in the perspective of God, the finite is seen not *in medias res* but in the overall vision of infinity. The evangelist, strong in the faith, expresses his vision by an initial literary device. By introducing the oddities of God-talk into his story, his story becomes more story-like: or we might say that his history becomes more history-like, less an actual reality and more of a reflection upon reality.

The narrative, then, has a narrator who may claim to be providing a literary-critical commentary upon his base material. Now, I do not believe that a story is essentially constructed in a logical sequence of cause and effect, so that one event or incident develops logically from its predecessor. You would find that a story told in this way would have a very peculiar, unreal and unfinished feel to it. Rather, the crucial developments in any story are essentially contingent, unexpected and even illogical. To take a very simple example, it is entirely unexpected and scandalous that immediately after Peter openly identifies the Messiah at Caesarea Philippi, Jesus should speak of his sufferings and death. The Messiah was supposed to be the great ruler of Israel, the saviour of the nation, and what he says seems nonsense.

But it is not nonsense in terms of the narrator's perspective, which is not intermediate and dependent upon a finite notion of cause and effect. The perspective is of an end which casts its shadow upon all intermediary preoccupations and gives a sense of meaning to the apparently contingent and jumbled narrative. The story of history becomes more story-like, more debatable and closer to the truth under the auspices of an intelligible end, beyond which it always projects itself so that the story may be seen as a whole by us who are in the midst of time. And in, and beyond, the end, there is God. This sense of an ending which is open to infinity accounts for the tendency of New Testament books to conclude with a projection beyond the limits of any possible historical reference. Thus, St. Matthew's Gospel concludes with the words, 'I am with you *always, to the end of time*' (28:20); St. John's Gospel: 'There is much else that Jesus did. If it were all to be recorded in detail, I suppose the whole world could not hold the books that would be written' (21:25); above all, the Revelation of John: 'Amen. *Come, Lord Jesus!*' (22:20). Yet it is in the nature of any good story to look past itself into a limitless future, in which everyone may *live happily ever after.*

If such is indeed in the nature of stories, and there is at the heart of the New Testament a primary urge to tell the story, then it becomes clear why it will not fit a static vision that is limited to the facts of history. Indeed the whole vision of the Bible moves forward in a progressive transformation from alienation to harmony. 'Listen!', writes St. Paul:

> I will unfold a mystery: we shall not all die, but we shall all be changed in a flash, in the twinkling of an eye, at the last trumpet-call. For the trumpet will sound, and the dead will rise immortal, and we shall be changed. This perishable being must be clothed with the imperishable, and what is mortal must be clothed with immortality.
>
> (I Corinthians 15:51–3)

Like Peter in his Pentecost sermon, Paul is writing about the victory over death that is achieved in Jesus Christ. His concern is *eschatalogical* – that is, about what comes at the end, and even beyond the end. But Paul, unlike Peter, is no longer directly referring to Jesus himself. In technical terms, the meaning of the story derives not from its *referential* but its *syntactical* force. In other words, what matters is the text before us rather than any history to which it refers.

On the other hand, I would not wish to make a false distinction between the Bible and the person of Christ. For in the metaphorical and imaginative literature of the New Testament they have become identified, and it is in the experience of this literature, and its development from and in worship, that we encounter Jesus the Christ.

THE UNITY AND COHERENCE OF THE NEW TESTAMENT

It is the eschatalogical nature of New Testament literature that finally requires us to be sensitive to its unity and coherence, and not to break it up into isolated fragments. This works at a number of levels. When reading the story of the Prodigal Son (Luke 15:11–32), we should not extract elements from it and endow them with any absolute significance. For each element, character and incident exists only in relation to the whole complex story, and whatever we derive from it is derived from our perception of the whole. Or at the level of a whole book, its 'good news' is properly heard in the resonances that echo from passage to passage. For example, the healing of the deaf man with the speech impediment in Mark 7:31–7 ought to be balanced with the healing of the blind man at Bethsaida (Mark 8:22–6), and both should be seen as commentaries upon the metaphorical deafness and blindness of the disciples, together with the fact that they themselves are μογιλάλοι (see Mark 7:32), that is, incapable of speaking clearly about Jesus. Then immediately after we see Jesus healing the deaf, the dumb and the blind, Peter at Caesarea Philippi for the first time perceives clearly and speaks plainly, stating boldly his belief in Jesus' Messiahship (Mark 8:29).

In such a way one could draw up a structured pattern for the whole of the Gospel. Ultimately, of course, it is infinitely complex and elusive, with all the oddities and contingencies of life itself, and I should not wish to fall foul of what in literary criticism has come to be known as the ' *intentional fallacy*', which would restrict interpretation to its author's conscious intentions for it. Great art, St. Mark's Gospel included, has a mystery, a richness and a complex unity which is far greater than the genius of one person.

Thirdly, I would ascribe this complex unity to the whole canon of the New Testament. There can be no simple answer to why these twenty-seven books should have been chosen to form the body of sacred scripture out of the many other writings of the early Christian era. Yet it remains a remarkable fact that this apparently miscellaneous collection of writing does reflect a unity in their common task of testifying to the transforming power of the Resurrection. All the more important, therefore, is their bewildering variety – as oddly many yet one as the Christian Church itself. Finally, therefore, I am brought back to my earlier point about the necessarily pluralistic interpretation of a literature which is itself so varied, and which is received by a society both complex and varied in the manner in which it attempts to interpret itself.

If nothing else, this will help us to realise that no interpretation of a text can be final, since not only is the text itself not simple, but it must gain meaning only in relationship to its readers, who will come to it from different contexts and with different critical equipment. While never denying that all in the end may be one, I shall conclude this chapter with one or two brief illustrations of this critical plurality from disciplines other than the purely literary.

ANTHROPOLOGY AND ARCHETYPES

Anthropologists, for example, may well wish to dispense altogether with the notion that the Bible is a record of history. More positively, then, they may characterise it as mytho-history such as they would encounter regularly in field research. Having suggested this structural similarity, anthropologists will proceed to employ upon the Bible those critical methods which they use in a more general interpretation of myth. For those of us with a more vested religious interest in the Bible, there will be loss as well as gain in such criticism. Yet there is no doubt that the anthropologist ought to be taken seriously by other kinds of biblical scholar.

From this approach we may proceed to the rather different treatment of archetype and myth as exemplified primarily in the work of the psychoanalyst Carl Jung, and I would not altogether dissociate such criticism from the sense of this chapter that the Bible can be regarded as one archetypal structure, a coherent mythology beginning with the creation and looking forward to the end of all things in God. The 'discovery' of the power of archetype and myth is not the achievement of modern psychoanalytical theory, but may be said to date from 1725 when the Italian Giambattista Vico published a book called *The New Science*. Vico's 'science' was the science of human society, at the heart of which is a *sapienza poetica* (poetic wisdom) which casts and orders society's environment. And so, for example, the great biblical 'myths' of creation – the garden of Eden, the flood, Cain and Abel – are not merely primitive stories. They were never intended to be taken as 'literally' true, but are highly sophisticated forms of encoding and describing human experience and its origins.

Myth is a way of grasping experience and making it manageable, and it is not inherently primitive. We continue to respond to and 'create' myths in the context of our changing experience of human society. This being the case, it is easy to see why the Bible suffers a perpetual process of demythologising, as the energies of modern people are engaged in creating new mythologies which they believe are more appropriate to contemporary social relations and human institutions. Obvious examples of such modern mythologies are Communism, Nazism and Fascism. Meanwhile, the inherited mythology of the Bible is rejected as primitive and childish.

I am not, therefore, terribly impressed when Jung claims to wish to preserve the proper expression of the 'natural religious function' of humanity. He does indeed deny that religion is simply an illusion, but by the drawing up of equivalences between the archetypes of the unconscious and the statements of religion, he reduces religious experience to a function of the human mind and society. There is, in the end, no room for God.

Let us see, then, what happens when this kind of analysis is applied to the text of the New Testament.

In truth, in very truth I tell you, a grain of wheat remains a solitary grain unless it falls into the ground and dies; but if it dies, it bears a rich harvest. The man who loves himself is lost, but he who hates himself in this world will be kept safe for eternal life.

(John 12:24–5)

But, how many ask, how are the dead raised? In what kind of body? How foolish! The seed you sow does not come to life unless it has first died; and what you sow is not the body that shall be, but a naked grain, perhaps of wheat, or of some other kind; and God clothes it with the body of his choice, each seed with its own particular body . . . So it is with the resurrection of the dead.

(I Corinthians 15:35–42)

I have deliberately chosen two very familiar passages. With

such it is all too easy to cloud our reading with the barrier of habit ingrained from childhood in school or church. As D. H. Lawrence wrote, the Bible 'is a book that has been temporarily killed for us, or for some of us, by having its meaning arbitrarily fixed . . . by old habit amounting almost to instinct it impresses on us a whole state of feeling'. Perhaps, therefore, we can awaken our responses afresh by regarding the New Testament from the psychoanalytical and mythological, rather than from the distinctively religious, standpoint. To begin with, then, we might make a correspondence between the image of the grain and a pattern in ancient poetic myth and ritual. Both the Greeks and the Egyptians used the idea of the corn, buried underground and then springing up, as a symbol of eternal life through death. The association of the New Testament text with such myths recalls us to the communal life which is revived, as opposed to the life of the individual upon which our modern sensibilities tend to focus. And so we see in the writings of St. Paul that the experience of oneness with Christ becomes through death a spiritual life which animates the whole body of believers (I Corinthians 15:48).

But now a note of reserve creeps in. Undoubtedly the author of the Fourth Gospel and St. Paul were concerned with the question of life in the future, beyond our present experience. The form of criticism which we are now employing, however, is limited to the present and actual, and the experience of eternal life as a *present* possession. The eschatalogical perspective is lost, and transcendence is precluded as an acceptable category. Difficulties increase as we read further in the gospel passage. Jesus foretells the manner of his death to the crowd.

> And I shall draw all men to myself, when I am lifted up from the earth.
>
> (John 12:32)

This looks back to the earlier prediction in John 3:14 that 'this Son of Man must be lifted up as the serpent was lifted up by Moses in the wilderness'. The image of the serpent, like the image of the grain, may be opened up to a variety of influences. Freudian analysis, for example, would suggest phallic symbolism, and an expression of the connection between the sense of guilt and fear and the anarchic impulses of sex. Associations cluster around the figure of the serpent; as a creature accursed (like Christ on the cross); or as one which sheds its skin (as Christ renewed life in putting off his old body). Where, though, does all this stop? The more I read of Freud and Jung as applied to the biblical literature, the more uneasy I become. Certainly Jung, above all, has demonstrated the wonder of the inner myth or story which is in each one of us and which is enlivened and illuminated within the context of the great stories of the world and above all, perhaps, the story of the gospels. Yet as the analysis is applied, it is found to be as sterile and as literal-minded as much traditional allegorical interpretation. Stories and images are denuded of intrinsic power as character and action take their significance only from the archetypal terms of psychoanalysis. Once again, there is a lack of proper attention to the text itself as its narrative is carved into a required shape and form.

Lastly, and very briefly, in addition to anthropology and psychoanalysis, philosophy can be a useful tool of biblical interpretation, used from the very earliest days and, indeed, an important element in certain strands of the New Testament itself. Greek philosophy plays its part in the Fourth Gospel with an odd amalgamation of Plato and the Stoics. The latter believed that all things in the universe were pervaded by Logos, regarded as a kind of general faculty of reason. Popular Platonism, which perhaps had very little to do with Plato himself, developed the idea of a real world which was ideal and perfect, of which the world we inhabit was a poor, soiled copy. Although our flesh may be tied to the earth, our minds may be purified to a contemplation of the Ideal, the Idea of the Good, or of God himself. It is not hard to see how early Christianity came to absorb such notions into its gospel and its accounts of Jesus Christ. Nor is it surprising that at Athens, St. Paul should have initiated an early and apparently constructive dialogue with the philosophers of the Areopagus (Acts 17:16–34). We too, in our day, will profit from a sensitivity to the voices of philosophy in our reading of the New Testament.

But as our critical boldness grows, we should become increasingly aware that we are posing ever more problems for the historicity of the Bible, and moving ever further away from the simple hope that we can trace from it an historical figure whom we shall recognise as our Saviour and Deliverer. This critical plurality may well have value in cleansing the New Testament of the religious paraphernalia of doctrinal creeds or theological propositions. But it has its own dangers, and I suggest that our best hope in this situation is to attend to the text as seriously as we may, as a coherent and responsible literary structure. Chapter 3, therefore, will seek to unpack this structure a little, examining how it works and the force of its language.

3 Imagination and Metaphor

FIGURATIVE AND LITERAL LANGUAGE

The word *metaphor* is derived directly from a Greek word 'μεταφέρω' which means 'I carry across'. In English it signifies a linguistic process whereby the characteristics of one object are 'carried across' and applied to another, so that the second object is spoken of in terms of the first. Such stretched language is called *figurative* – language which does not mean what is says. (This should not be confused with the method of figural interpretation described in the previous chapter.)

> 'And some of the seed fell into good soil, where it came up and grew, and bore fruit; and the yield was thirtyfold, sixtyfold, even a hundredfold.' He added, 'If you have ears to hear, then hear.'
>
> (Mark 4:8–9)

We are not really being told about the state of the farmer's crops. Figurative language interferes with the literal reference of the words – seed, soil, fruit – and carries them across into a new, wider sphere. Another sort of metaphor which is frequently used in the parables is the *simile*, in which the transference is proposed and explained with a word such as 'like'.

> How shall we picture the kingdom of God, or by what parable shall we describe it? It is like the mustard-seed,

27

which is smaller than any seed in the ground at its sowing. But once sown, it springs up and grows taller than any other plant, and forms branches so large that the birds can settle in its shade.

(Mark 4:30–2)

If figurative language interferes with the ordinary connections of words and their referents, *literal* language means what it says, or at least intends to, so that literally the parable of the sower refers to no more than a man sowing his field and watching his crops grow up. But we should not assume, therefore, that literal language bears a closer relation to the truth than figurative language. We may compare, for example, these two verses:

For all who are moved by the Spirit of God are sons of God.

(Romans 8:14)

When he had gone a little further he saw James son of Zebedee.

(Mark 1:19)

Clearly those in the first category are not 'sons' in the same way as James is a son of his natural father. Yet that need not render meaningless or untrue their description as sons of God. In short, the terms figurative (or metaphorical) and literal describe different types of language, both of which may be true in their own particular way.

Now the natural language of parables being figurative, it is almost inevitable that human beings who like to get things straight, to be literally clear, and to iron their religion out into the conceptual clarity of doctrinal creeds, will feel uncomfortable with them. But I believe that a long history of interpretation has shielded us from the lurking suspicion that the parables are meant to make us feel uncomfortable. Commentators and interpreters will try to straighten out the riddle of the parable, to define its meaning according to their theology or creed. But the disquieting riddle was there from the start. In chapter 1 I referred to Mark's mysterious account of the purpose of parables, and it now warrants a closer look.

> When he was alone, the Twelve and others who were round him questioned him about the parables. He replied, 'To you the secret of the kingdom of God has been given; but to those who are outside everything comes by way of parables, so that (as Scripture says) they may look and look, but see nothing; they may hear and hear, but understand nothing; otherwise they might turn to God and be forgiven.'
>
> (Mark 4:10–12)

The earliest commentator on the text – assuming that St. Mark's Gospel is given chronological priority – is St. Matthew, who apparently attempted to overcome the problem of Jesus' deliberate mystification of the people by replacing 'so that' (ἵνα) with 'for' (ὅτι) (Matthew 13:13). Matthew's revision is clearly an attempt to draw the sting out of a difficult text rather an attention to the difficulty itself. Modern critics in their turn have constructed elaborate theories which side-step the linguistic and literary difficulties of accepting the text of Mark as it stands. Yet what does it convey to those who are prepared to exercise a willing suspension of disbelief? Perhaps its scandal and its enigmatic quality is quite deliberate, posing a riddle which yields no simple interpretation and requires an exercise of the imagination. It may, indeed, be a mistake to look for information to be revealed in the dark sayings and parables, for their sense may lie in the mysterious nature of the riddle itself. Perhaps the scandal and the enigma is at the very heart of the gospel, and to rationalise it away would be to dissolve the essence of scripture. Like the disciples we are continually challenged with the question, 'Do you still not understand?' The pattern, indeed, invites but does not force an underlying meaning to be discerned, and the text may be, by nature, jealous of the precious treasure that it guards. During this and the next chapter, let us suspend our desire to make sense of and derive meaning from the text and simply see what is happening in the narratives and metaphors of the figurative language of the New Testament. We need to see how language works before we can begin to define what information it may communicate.

ARISTOTLE AND THE LANGUAGE OF POETRY

It may be helpful to begin with Aristotle again. He distinguished three categories in the arts of language: logic, rhetoric and poetic. Each has its own particular purpose, and the distinction between them is largely a matter of metaphor. Very briefly, 'clarity' and the ability to persuade and change our opinions are the functions of logic and rhetoric. Poetic, on the other hand, is both imitative and metaphorical, has 'distinctiveness' rather than 'clarity', and by moving beyond the realms of 'ordinary' speech, does not seek so much to persuade as to invite us to use our imaginations, engaging both our hearts and minds. Consider this familiar passage from Revelation:

> Then I saw a new heaven and a new earth, for the first heaven and the first earth had vanished, and there was no longer any sea. I saw the holy city, new Jerusalem, coming down out of heaven from God, made ready like a bride adorned for her husband. I heard a loud voice proclaiming from the throne: 'Now at last God has his dwelling among

men! He will dwell among them and they shall be his people, and God himself will be with them. He will wipe every tear from their eyes; there shall be an end to death, and to mourning and crying and pain; for the old order has passed away!'

(Revelation 21:1–4)

That fulfils well Aristotle's notion of the poetic. There is certainly no attempt at persuasion. It is imitative, drawing upon our store of familiar images, and it is, above all, metaphorical, for it can hardly claim to mean what it says, with cities floating down and loud proclamatory voices. 'Ordinary' speech has clearly been abandoned.

But we cannot afford to be pedantic and academic as we read such a passage. What is more important is to receive it gratefully as an immensely moving, lovely and consoling piece of writing. Why does it have this extraordinary power to stir the heart and comfort the sorrowful? Well, to begin with, it has in abundance the Aristotelian quality of 'distinctiveness'. It resonates to the sadnesses of life, death and bereavement, and precisely draws the act of comfort – the wiping of the tearful eye. It neither promises comfort, nor expresses sympathy; it acts effectively. Equally distinctive are the images of earth and heaven. They do not need to be described in the language of 'clarity'. They are images lodged deep in our imaginations and inner selves to begin with, and it is simple, sharp words that give a new edge to the familiar: 'new', 'vanished', 'has passed away'. There is no room for 'perhaps' or 'maybe': the mystery of 'God with us' has changed everything.

I keep the word mystery, for I do not suggest that what I have said solves any of the problems of this passage from Revelation, and to a large extent these are problems of language. As I am always insisting, our primary attention is demanded by the text, and the text is a linguistic construct.

It should be clear to start with that reference to observable and verifiable objects, persons or events is not necessarily essential for language to be meaningful. Meaning, indeed, may have to be hunted for in much more devious and elusive ways. Then there is a powerful tradition in Western thought which suggests that clarity should not necessarily be regarded as the principal purpose of the act of thinking. The poetic distinctiveness of Revelation properly allows for what is indistinct and even unclear in its metaphorical, imaginative language, within a work of art which requires an energetic exercise of the mind and intelligence. This very exercise is an indissoluble combination of seeing into the very heart of things and of creating the images which grant us such perception. What is most 'true' in literature, then, is not necessarily derived from what is actually seen and observed, but from what is cast in the furnace of the perceptive and prophetic imagination. Nor should language which is primarily metaphorical and imaginative be regarded as less serious or grounded in matters of basic concern than that which claims to have the authority of scientific or historical verification. Finally, I suggest that it is a characteristic of such language that it bears not one meaning or significance but many. Unlike the language of science, which would prefer to eliminate the problems and uncertainties of multiple meanings (what is technically known as *polysemy*), the language of metaphor and the imagination welcomes the creative use of polysemy, as throwing light on the mystery and inexhaustibility of its subject. Certainly when an author writes with a clear intention, as the evangelists or St. Paul did, this at least implies (without falling prey to the 'intentional fallacy') a normative meaning within the limits of their intention. Nevertheless, within these limits interpretations may be many. Indeed, ultimately there may never be one right interpretation of the New Testament or even of any one book within it.

I would dare to suggest that we would do well to regard the four evangelists, St. Paul, the author of Revelation and one or two other New Testament writers as poets. There is a long tradition in many literatures, our own included, that the poet is one inspired with a mission to communicate to mankind the workings of divinity, and that poetry is a channel for divine revelation. Furthermore, Samuel Taylor Coleridge, one of our greatest poets and literary critics, suggested that the faculty of the human imagination was the equivalent of the divine act of creation. It is the primary and creative agent of human perception and expression.

There are some very clear examples of 'poetic' writing in the New Testament, as apparent in the Greek as in English translations. I Timothy 3:16 appears to be a quotation from an early Christian verse or hymn:

> He who was manifested in the body,
>> vindicated in the spirit,
>> seen by angels;
> who was proclaimed among the nations,
>> believed in throughout the world,
>> glorified in high heaven.

The six lines may be arranged in various ways: as three couplets, six parallel single lines, or two three-lined strophes. But they are undeniably written under the formal conditions of verse, of metre, parallelism, and so on. Being bound by such conditions, language is allowed to break across barriers of sense and logic, so that the man who is seen quite naturally in the flesh (ἐν σαρκί), is seen also by the non-human, heavenly eyes of angels (ἀγγέλοις). He who is believed in throughout the human world (ἐν κόσῳ) is worshipped also in the heavenly world (ἐν δόξῃ). Imagination here ranges freely across the worlds of flesh and spirit, controlled by the structure of the verse.

Here is another example of the poetry of the New Testament, from Matthew 7:13–14

Enter by the narrow gate.

> The gate is wide that leads to perdition,
>   there is plenty of room on the road,
>   and many go that way;
>
>   but the gate that leads to life is small
>   and the road is narrow,
>   and those who find it are few.

The balancing of ideas is short phrases is typical of Old Testament, Hebrew poetry, while 'walking in the right path' is a common metaphor in Jewish teaching (see Psalms I; 119; Isaiah 55:6–9; *inter alia*). As I have set the poem out, it is easy to see its structure of balance and contrast, and also the radical nature of its images. The one road is wide with *plenty* of room, the other almost as narrow as can be. This quality of the poetic language of the New Testament which cuts away irrelevances and stretches its images to a simple, unequivocal sharpness, will be looked at more closely in the next chapter. Its very distinctiveness brings home to us, the readers of the text, the decision which the metaphor or narrative demands.

My third example of 'poetic' writing is again from the Revelation of John.

> I turned to see whose voice it was that spoke to me; and when I turned I saw seven standing lamps of gold, and among the lamps one like a son of man, robed down to his feet, with a golden girdle round his breast. The hair of his head was white as snow-white wool, and his eyes flamed like fire; his feet gleamed like burnished brass refined in a furnace, and his voice was like the sound of rushing waters. In his right hand he held seven stars, and out of his mouth came a sharp two-edged sword; and his face shone like the sun in full strength.

> (Revelation 1:12–16)

This description of the Son of Man is full of Old Testament phrases and references, and it is tempting to play the commentator's game of tracking down allusions, pedantically unravelling their significance and establishing their original context. But the art of Revelation is more than simply an *allegorical* code in which each symbol and item requires exact translation into prosaic equivalent, so that the white hair means this and the flaming eyes mean that. Rather, the whole description, redolent of the Old Testament, should be taken together as an indivisible entity of great emotive and evocative power. It is not intended to have the clarity of a portrait, but it is distinctive in its sense of awe and majesty, age and authority, sublimity and glory. Our imaginations respond readily to this metaphorical vision of the divine, and it is right that it should be so.

There are, of course, enormous difficulties in the attempt to distinguish between the procedures of poetic inspiration and the work of divine inspiration and revelation as it operates in a poetic mind like that of the author of the Revelation of John. Not all great poetry is 'religious', and the imagination can certainly function without reference to the fundamental mystery of divine inspiration. Yet it remains true that there is much in common between the practice of the prophet (and Jesus himself is frequently linked in the New Testament with the great Hebrew prophetic tradition) and the poet, and between the secular poet and the religious seer. I have briefly referred, for example, to some of the controls which poetry may exert on language, such as metre, rhythm or perhaps rhyme. The formality which these require present an imaginative challenge to both writer and reader, so that the resultant harmony of a well wrought poem or narrative becomes a kind of verbal music which reaches levels in us far deeper than the merely conscious or intellectual, and yet demands a response which is fully intelligent and alert.

I would root this imaginative challenge that is presented by poetry and divine inspiration in their common projection in images which are finally irreducible and untranslatable, but are alive with an inexhaustible significance. Inasmuch as metaphor is a 'carrying across', their metaphorical nature is the agent which draws together things hitherto dispersed and disparate. The Messiah eats with publicans and sinners; a despised Samaritan becomes the good neighbour; 'through faith you are all sons of God in union with Christ Jesus' (Galatians 3:26). In the poetic language of the imagination, the many are carried and drawn together as the one. And where the imagination works together with the inspired belief that the Creator everywhere underlies and encourages the creature, the peculiar poetry and authority of the New Testament writers becomes evident. Their imagination will be found to partake of the transforming power of the Resurrection itself.

GOD AND RELIGIOUS LANGUAGE

But lest our conclusions should begin to seem rather too triumphant, we should not abandon or deny the very real difficulties of religious language, including the language of the New Testament. The difficulties arise, not least, from the fact that those people who would invest any real weight of belief in it are an ever-dwindling minority. Where is its cutting edge? Perhaps, then, we should dwell for a moment at the point where religious language begins, in the word 'God'. The word can be said or used in an enormous variety of contexts, sacred and profane, reverently and blasphemously, but is it in any way adequate to express the reality of God, he of whom the creeds speak? No doubt many of us have got little further than A. A. Milne's Elizabeth Ann in *Now We Are Six*, who asked her nurse how God began. Not surprisingly she failed to get a satisfactory answer, and so she conceived the rash plan to 'run round the world till she found a man/Who knew *exactly* how God began'.

I suggest that we will only make a proper start in the quest when, New Testament in hand, we come to terms with the idea of metaphor and metaphorical language. For, first of all, metaphor is open to a plurality of perspectives and interpretation which allows us, on the one hand, to exist honestly in the pluralistic society of which I have spoken in earlier chapters, and on the other, to avoid the destructive limitations which any one model or concept of God places upon our sense of divinity. Metaphorical language is accustomed to speaking about great mysteries of life – the common themes of poetry are love, mortality, joy, friendship, hatred. It is therefore well suited to talking about the greatest mystery of all. And since metaphor is so much a part of our speech (without thinking we speak of 'golden hair' and 'cherry lips'), we might forget that metaphors can be shocking in the way they draw together the dissimilar, jolting our imaginations with ideas of the Kingdom of Heaven in terms of lost coins, mustard seeds and buried treasure. Are we prepared to let the New Testament disturb and even shock our vague but no doubt relatively comfortable idea of God? Let it speak for itself:

Divine folly is wiser than the wisdom of man.

(I Corinthians 1:25)

God is our father, and God alone.

(John 8:41)

For our God is a devouring fire.

(Hebrews 12:29)

For God is love.

(I John 4:8)

> . . . and on the throne sat one whose appearance was like the gleam of jasper and cornelian; and round the throne was a rainbow, bright as an emerald.
>
> (Revelation 4:3)

God, then, is foolish yet also brilliantly glorious; a father, a destructive fire, love itself. He is all these things, and no one of them is adequate to describe him. Each image of him enlarges a little our imaginative reach, yet we are always left with a feeling of inadequacy. Whatever image we may use is both true and untrue, for if we see God as Father, we need also to see him as King, and if King then also Creator, and if Creator then also the God of vengeance, and of love, and so on, *ad infinitum*.

I suggest that the word 'God' actually stands outside ordinary language altogether. In fact I suspect that it is only really comfortable in the context of worship and prayer, but that would take me far beyond my present subject. From our New Testament examples we have derived more of an interrelated structure than a picture for God, and this idea of a structure encourages a multiplicity of images, some of which may be very disturbing to our established, central notions about God. By extension the numerous parables of the Kingdom of God in the gospels offer an extremely complex and elusive sense of the nature of God and his rule. We shall look at the parables more closely in the next chapter.

But it is not enough to say that religious language and language about God requires a metaphorical structure of multiple images which perpetually stretch our minds and imaginations. Recall the poetic description of Christ in I Timothy 3:16. He is seen in the flesh, and also by angels. He is proclaimed throughout the nations of the world, and glorified in heaven. Our eyes and voices could not perform all of these functions, for they are limited to the fleshly and the mundane. The language of sight and speech is being used on two quite distinct levels, one familiar to our experience, the other realised only in our imaginations. Now this odd mixing of 'language levels' happens all the time in religious discourse. It is actually what gives it its oddity and cutting edge, and our problem all too often is that we make such discourse too normal, too sane, and too safe.

Most of us use a range of 'language levels' in our everyday lives, and we are experts in keeping them apart. There is a language for the pulpit, a language for the lecture hall, a language for the pub and a language for the children. We switch from one to another with unconscious ease, but we become painfully aware when a language level slips into the wrong context. I suggest that frequently in the New Testament, such language levels are deliberately fused so as to prompt an oddity in talk of God and our relationship with the divine. It makes us feel uncomfortable and opens up the rational limits of our minds and imagination. The religious language of Scripture tolerates a strangeness which everyday speech would reject, and in this way makes it possible for us to discern and reflect upon something of the strange mystery of God and his incarnation in Christ.

Consider the threefold question put to Peter at the end of the Fourth Gospel, balancing his earlier threefold denial of Christ before the crucifixion. I am conscious that many modern commentators would disagree with my interpretation of the two words used for 'love', preferring to regard them as synonyms. But I am persuaded that my understanding at least has the merit of attending closely to the language of the text and taking its nuances seriously and at face value.

> After breakfast, Jesus said to Simon Peter, 'Simon son of John do you love (ἀγαπᾷς) me more than all else?' 'Yes, Lord,' he answered, 'you know that I love (φιλῶ) you.' 'Then feed my lambs,' he said. A second time he asked, 'Simon son of John, do you love (ἀγαπᾷς) me?' 'Yes, Lord, you know I love (φιλῶ) you.' 'Then tend my sheep.' A third time he said, 'Simon son of John, do you love

(φιλεῖς) me?' 'Peter was hurt that he asked him a third
time, 'Do you love (φιλεῖς) me?' 'Lord,' he said, you
know everything, you know I love (φιλῶ) you.' Jesus said,
'Feed my sheep.'

(John 21:15–17)

The tension of the dialogue depends partly on the insistent
repetition of the questions, but partly on the deliberate
rubbing together of the words φιλέω and ἀγαπάω. Jesus
begins with the strong word which we still associate with the
Church in our term 'agape'. Peter replies affirmatively, but
with the weaker term for love, implying perhaps no more
than a human affection and caring. He will not commit
himself to the final and deeply religious commitment which
is suggested by Jesus' question. The second question and
answer repeats this pattern. But then in his third question,
Jesus himself employs the weaker term. Perhaps we might
paraphrase his words as, 'Can you claim even to care for
me?' Brought to this point, Peter can no longer offer a reply,
but only trust in Jesus' knowledge of him.

Throughout this searching conversation, Jesus keeps re-
peating to Peter the words of his commission, 'Feed my
sheep'. Peter, humbled by his threefold denial and his threefold confession, is still the instrument for his Lord's work.
His self-realisation is achieved in the deliberate bringing
together of two levels of language in the terms, 'αγάπη' – a
divine commitment which Christ makes possible – and 'φιλία'
– a human affection between friends. This self-realisation
brings about a stronger and more humble knowledge of the
human relationship with the Lord, and finally a clearer sense
of God himself. In the first instance Peter simply could not
bear the implications of Jesus' words. It was language in the
wrong context. Yet its deliberate use jolted him into a new
humility and a new realism.

THE IMAGINATION AND HISTORY

The last two chapters have been mainly concerned with the New Testament as history and as imaginative writing. Not for one moment would I suggest that these are mutually exclusive. Indeed, just as the authors of scripture needed to keep a balance between imaginative art and its historical origins, so its readers must similarly balance an imaginative reconstruction and commitment with a careful sensitivity to the historical milieu of the writing and its subject. There are here three parties involved in the exercise (four, if we include the Holy Spirit): the writer, the text and the reader. I hope by now it is clear that I have abandoned the simple notion that the reader should swallow whole everything the author puts into the text, like John eating his scroll in Revelation 10:10. Rather, it is an exercise in which complex and sometimes challenging relationships are set up between author, text and reader, and interpretation depends as much upon the reader's perspective and strategy as almost anything else. That is partly why interpretation is so difficult. It makes a difference where you 'place' yourself in the narrative – with the prodigal son or his brother at home, with the Pharisee congratulating himself in the temple, or with the publican? (Luke 15:11–12; 18:10–14). Most of us will vacillate uneasily and uncomfortably.

This exercise is called, in literary criticism and theology, *hermeneutics*, or the theory of the interpretation of texts. More precisely it is the science of interpretation which begins with the attempt to explain the original sense of the text (*exegesis*), and proceeds to expound its relevance for modern readers (*exposition*). Even this definition leaves me a little uneasy in so far as it suggests that the text can be trapped into meaning something and then served up in a digestible form in sermon or study group. Let me therefore sound a final note of caution, with a plea for the use of the imagination.

Critics engaged in the hermeneutic exercise quickly become familiar with what is often referred to as the *hermeneutic circle*. Initially we bring to our reading of a text, a gospel or an epistle, a set of presuppositions or assumptions about it which enable us to make some sense of what is being said. Thus we may read the opening of St. Paul's letter to the Galatians: 'I am astonished to find you turning so quickly away from him who called you by grace, and following a different gospel.' (1:6). Before we can even begin to understand this verse, we need to make some presuppositions about the gospel which Paul wishes to defend. In the light of those we can enter into a form of dialogue with the text of his letter, which no doubt will cause an enlargement of our understanding and enable us to re-read the text on the basis of a new awareness of its assumptions. The process may be repeated many times in an apparently circular movement of assumption – text revised – assumption, and interpretation may seem simply to be turning in on itself. If, however, in practice it works, it is because there remains at the heart of good interpretation what German critics in the nineteenth century called *Verstehen*, an insight and intuition which is present in the initial act of reading and remains through each stage of revision and interpretation. My term for it would be the imagination.

4 The Story Told

THE PROBLEM OF NARRATIVE: THE FOURTH GOSPEL

Contemporary studies in 'narrative theology' are many, and their number grows daily. On the whole I do not find them very helpful, and I have mentioned one or two of the most useful in my Reading List. There are two principal short-comings in most of these works. On the one hand many of them use the idea of 'story' as an easy way out of giving serious attention to the problems of the New Testament. There is, however, nothing simple or naïve in the idea of 'story' or 'narrative'. On the other hand, many fail to perceive the extremely difficult relationship between 'narrative' – the telling of a story – and theology. I shall return to this in more detail later in this chapter. First I want to continue in the manner and tone of my previous chapter, with a specific and detailed look at the text of one book of the New Testament.

Reading these scriptural narratives demands not an assault upon the text with the purpose of extracting its meaning to be packaged in creed and proposition, but a sensitive awareness of what is dramatically happening and what is happening to readers as they experience the metaphors, tensions and interrelationships of the language and story.

Let us apply a critical approach through the structures of story and narrative to the Fourth Gospel, taking first a general perspective, and then a specific look at one detail of the writing. For some time now we have become accustomed to regarding this Gospel as a literary whole, a dramatic unity

43

constructed on the basis of symmetrical design and balanced units. It combines close attention to visual and historical detail, and sharp, sometimes heavily ironic, speech, with broad cross-references in image and incident. Such detail and patterns may be found also in the narratives of the Old Testament and the Apocrypha, in Ruth, Esther and Judith. The Fourth Gospel is heir to an ancient Hebrew tradition.

In brief, the Gospel is shaped by the evangelist's dramatic vision of the words and life of Jesus, and in his various encounters – with Nicodemus (3:1–21), with the Samaritan woman (4:1–30), with Pontius Pilate (18:28–19:22), and so on – this is blended with their effect on those around him. Throughout there is a bifocal reference to the life of Jesus Christ and the life of the community. But more than that, the drama of Jesus' encounters prompts an interpretative response from the reader. Invariably, there is something very strange about the discussions: that Nicodemus, a learned and famous teacher, should ask such questions of Jesus; that Jesus, a rabbi, should be talking with a woman, and a Samaritan woman at that; strangest of all is Jesus' dialogue with Pilate at his trial, which I shall be looking at more closely in a moment. All the time readers are being thrown off balance, so that they cannot read simply as spectators. They become involved in the text, adjusting the focus and pitch, negotiating the implications of discussions carried out under such odd conditions. They begin to play an active role in making these adjustments, and that is exactly what is intended in the narrative. Its bifocal reference, then, to the life of Jesus and the community, is effective not only for the disciples and controversialists who people the Gospel, but for the person and community which reads it now, and for those who will read it tomorrow.

The narrative unfolds thematically upon the life of Christ. Chapters 1 – 5 focus upon the image of water, and Jesus as the source of life. The next three chapters change to the image of blood, with Jesus as life's preserver in the midst of a threatening world. In the central section of the Gospel the

images of light and life are explored in the incidents of the
healing of the blind man and the raising of Lazarus. Then
the long discourses of the Last Supper play upon the Spirit of
love and counsel. Finally, in Jesus' death and resurrection,
as all prophecies are fulfilled, the Christian who has been
drawn progressively into the texture of the narrative by its
literary devices of irony and surprise and discontinuity, is
finally identified with the pattern of the Incarnation: through
baptism, eucharist, the Spirit, and finally by death into new
light and life.

So much for a broad perspective on the story of the Fourth
Gospel. Let us now glimpse one of those literary devices in
action. Jesus' response to the questions of Pilate is a remarkable example of what literary critics call *discontinuous dialogue.* Here it is, set out like a play script:

PILATE: Are you the king of the Jews?

JESUS: Is that your own idea, or have others suggested
          it to you?

PILATE: What! am I a Jew? Your own nation and their
          chief priests have brought you before me. What
          have you done?

JESUS: My kingdom does not belong to this world. If it
          did, my followers would be fighting to save me
          from arrest by the Jews. My kingly authority
          comes from elsewhere.

PILATE: You are a king, then?

JESUS: 'King' is your word. My task is to bear witness
          to the truth. For this I was born; for this I came
          into the world, and all who are not deaf to truth
          listen to my voice.

PILATE: What is truth?

(from John 18:33–8)

Pilate never gets a straight answer to his question. Indeed, by the end, all the assumptions and agreed references which lie behind his line of enquiry have been utterly overthrown, so that he himself is, in a sense, the defendant and not Jesus. His first question is simply thrown back at him. His second question could not be plainer, 'What have you done?' In reply, Jesus now answers the first question, but obliquely. He does not reply that he *is* a king, but that his kingdom is not of the kind known to Pilate. Pilate is confused and tries his first question again. '*Are* you a king?' Again, Jesus side-steps, and speaks of his work rather than his status. Then follows Pilate's last and most famous question.

The effect of all this upon the reader is similar to the dislocating effect of Jesus' earlier encounters, but now considerably amplified . On the one hand we can recognise with some satisfaction that the tables have been turned on Pilate who, thinking he is in control, is totally out of his depth. But more significantly, far from being accordingly granted a sharper perspective on a masterful Jesus, we find that he is always slipping out of focus, the discontinuities in the dialogue preventing us from establishing him as the strongly defined hero. Indeed, by the narrative, we are prevented from holding Jesus as a dramatic character in a clear relationship, so that we are made to feel a perpetual sense of reaching out to a universe of discourse which is here only hinted at, and to a realm which utterly transcends the assumptions underlying all such perfectly reasonable questions as those of Pilate.

CONFUSION AND MYSTERY

Shifting language, the blurring of concept, the shaking of assumptions – all these lively things were claimed for the novel by that most lively and disturbing story-teller, D. H. Lawrence. He set large store by his art.

To be alive, to be man alive, to be whole man alive: that is the point . . . And only in the novel are *all* things given full play, or at least, they may be given full play, when we realise that life itself, and not inert safety, is the reason for living. For out of the full play of all things emerges the only thing that is anything, the wholeness of a man, the wholeness of a woman, man alive, and live woman.

Lawrence described the Bible as 'a great confused novel'. Quite simply, the Bible is the book of life, and its vitality arises out of its inclusiveness and its limitless openness to ordinary life. In the end it may well be futile to ask why the young man in the linen cloth is in St. Mark's Gospel, or why Mark interrupted his account of Jesus' ministry to describe in graphic detail the circumstances of the murder of John the Baptist. Why try to smooth them out with subtle reasoning? Perhaps they are simply a part of the fractured, pierced surface of the work of art, flaws reflecting the flaws of life itself. They are why one can say of this novel what the Dubliner said of James Joyce's *Ulysses*: 'We're all in the bloody book'. In the New Testament, that confused, baggy monster of a novel, we discover the unutterable particularity of experience, and that the novel being about people (and one person especially) is inevitably random, accidental and liable to break out of formal plans and patterns.

St. Mark's Gospel is both funny and tragic, infinitely complex and elusive, like life itself. The great tragedy of the Passion narrative is balanced against the comic thick-headedness of the disciples (e.g. 8:21, 9:34). Of course, ecclesiastical institution and popular piety struggle to prevent us from reading the Gospel in this uninhibited and fundamentally realistic way, and that is a great pity. For to acknowledge that the narrative is flawed and broken by seemingly incidental and informal bits and pieces need not entail us in suggesting that it is therefore without shape and coherence. I assume that the New Testament writers of narrative wrote for and expected thoughtful and intelligent readers who would enter into the life of the stories, making subtle connections and illuminating their reading from the apparently broken fragments, so that what is contingent is found to be necessary to the whole elaborate and infinitely mysterious design.

Such a reading demands faith, and on those who remain obstinately outside such faith art resolutely closes its doors and guards its secrets. The ἵνα of Mark 4:12 means what it says. But this alliance of literature with truth and truth with faith does not essentially involve a religious or pious attitude. 'I have faith', cried the father of the epileptic boy, 'help me where faith falls short' (Mark 9:24). Many poets and writers are familiar with the experience of believing beyond belief, searching in hope, like the desperate father, out of misery and confusion.

What the text demands of us is an authentic response, and that in itself is an act of faith and belief. As the writer seeks for truth, he appeals primarily not to our common sense, wisdom, intelligence or credulity. What he requires is a willing suspension of disbelief and an act of faith and hope that allows him to awaken in the hearts of his readers a sense of the wholeness of people, the solidarity of humanity, and the reality of the transforming power of Christ, crucified and risen.

THE RELIGIOUS USE OF STORY

Having said all this, it is odd that there is no word in the New Testament for story. Perhaps the nearest we can get is the distinction made in I Timothy 4:7–9 between μῦθος and λόγος, which is derived from the classical authors Pindar and Plato. In that passage Christians are warned against βεβήλοι μύθοι ('godless myths') which are 'fit only for old women', since as Christians they deal with πιστὸς ὁ λόγος ('the true story'). But no doubt the difficulty in identifying the particular form of 'story' in the New Testament should warn us against being too anxious to define critically and academically what a story *is*. If you want a structural analysis of the story, I suggest that you will not do better than consult once again Aristotle's *On the Art of Poetry*. There is, however, no simple answer to the question, and while I have made one or two suggestions in chapter 2 (see pp. 18–19), I prefer here to look at two important ways in which story is *used* in the New Testament.

I have already referred briefly to the debate about whether the Last Supper was a Passover meal or not. For now I will assume that it was, simply because there is a text which directly tells us so: 'How I have longed to eat this Passover with you before my death!' (Luke 22:15). The Passover was at the heart of Jewish worship and no doubt its origins lie in an agricultural setting. But its character as it was celebrated in Jesus' time is made clear from Deuteronomy 16:3.

> For seven days you shall eat unleavened cakes, the bread of affliction. In urgent haste you came out of Egypt, and thus as long as you live you shall commemorate the day of your coming out of Egypt.

The Passover was a commemoration of the Exodus. Part of the ritual of the Passover meal, still practised today, was an interpretation of the elements of the meal. A member of the family, usually the son, asked its head to describe the peculiar nature of the meal, and the reply came in the form of a story, based on Deuteronomy 26:5–11, and recounting the events of the Exodus. Now this story told to commemorate the escape of the Israelites from Egypt was not simply descriptive, but its repetition brought the power of the founding reality into the present and looked forward to Israel's vindication in the future. The events remembered in the story are related to past, present and future, and at each Passover those at the meal in a sense relive the ancient release from bondage.

Anthropologists and sociologists of religion suggest that some such use of narrative is a common feature of religious festivals. The story is linked with a fundamental experience of the society – marriage, birth, death, the approach of spring, and harvest – and its ritual repetition revives the original power of the experience and its interpretation in the narrative. Death, perhaps, is overcome in some mythic struggle.

The importance of this religious use of story for the Christian gospel cannot be overestimated. In the Eucharist we 'remember his offering of himself made once for all upon the cross', the telling of a unique story in a present re-enactment. At the heart of the sacrament is what we have come to know as the *institution narrative*, drawn straight from the gospels and from St. Paul.

> . . .the Lord Jesus, on the night of his arrest, took bread and, after giving thanks to God, broke it and said: 'This is my body, which is for you; do this as a memorial of me (εἰς τὴν ἐμὴν ἀνάμνησιν). In the same way, he took the cup after supper, and said: 'This cup is the new covenant sealed by my blood. Whenever you drink it, do this as a memorial of me'. For every time you eat this bread and drink the cup, you proclaim the death of the Lord, until he comes.

> (I Corinthians 11:23–6)

As it was with the Jewish Passover, so it is with the Christian Eucharist: the history of salvation is realised afresh in the repetition of the story, which is re-enacted, in the action of eating and drinking, in the lives of those who tell and hear it. As in any good story, we become active participants in it, and if story is a selective representation and heightening of human experience, it is also, in the New Testament, religious proclamation.

THE PARABLES

This brings me to a consideration of a second important way in which story is used, in the parables of the gospels. For in then, again, we inescapably play our part. There cannot be many stories more familiar to us than that which we have come to call 'The Prodigal Son' (Luke 15:11–32). For sheer economy and narrative brilliance it has few rivals. As you read it, therefore, simply allow the power of the story to play upon you. Never try to match up characters or elements in the story with people or things outside its structure. That is to treat it as *allegory*, whose meaning is extrinsic to the story. But this parable is an extended metaphor demanding an exclusive attention to an involvement in its language and the rhythms of its interior structure, for its power lies within the story. Yet as the language is stretched in its metaphorical usage, its sense is not exhausted by the human situation and an infinite perspective begins to illuminate its network of worldly relationships, joys and sorrows. Finite and infinite are drawn together by the power of words.

It is a story of all or nothing. The younger son turns the *whole* of his share of the estate into cash. He spends it *all* in reckless living. His poverty and hunger are so great that he would have been glad to eat pig-swill, but *no one* gave him *anything*. On his return home, the reversal of fortune is total. His father sends for his *best* robe and kills a fatted calf – a great extravagance in a country where meat was a rarity. Again, the elder brother's reaction is extreme to the point of absurdity. This radical nature of the story-telling, with its extremes of baseness, incredible forgiveness and violent jealousy, works strongly upon the reader who cannot help but identify in some way with the story, responding to it emotionally and finding him or herself in the foolishness, the recklessness, the jealousy and perhaps the humility. The reader's response is governed by a linguistic style that is stretched to the point where the images of human life break through into a perception of a greater love and a greater forgiveness. Thus the metaphor works. It would be an impoverishment to extract from it maxim or proposition which might suggest that the parable is 'about' God's boundless love, or some other abstraction. Rather the story propels us beyond our present condition towards new insights into the nature of love itself, by images at once familiar and yet utterly radical. If it has meaning it is in the image and figurative language and not in some abstract translation from them.

The word 'parable' is derived from the Greek 'παρα-βάλλω', which means 'to cast by the side of', or, metaphorically, 'to compare'. In the parables of Jesus, the kingdom of God is described in metaphors and similes, one thing spoken of in terms of another. The Greeks understood perfectly this sense of the parable, yet the antecedents of the New Testament form lie not in the Greek tradition but in Jewish literature and the Old Testament. The Hebrew *mašal* was not merely in story form and covers almost any verbal image or figurative saying. It embraces the forms of metaphor, riddle, proverb, allegory, parabolic story, and many others. Amos's basket of ripe summer fruit (Amos 8:1–3), the proverb, 'Is Saul also among the prophets?' (I Samuel 19:24) and Nathan's narrative parable told to David (II Samuel 12:1–4) all fall within the category of *mašal*. Similarly, in the New Testament the word 'παραβολή' is used to mean a comparison (Luke 5:36), a riddle (Mark 7:17), or just a straightforward rule (Luke 14:7). In fact, if you look carefully at the great 'parables' of St. Luke's Gospel, the stories of the Prodigal Son, the Good Samaritan, or the Dishonest Steward, you will rarely find them described by the evangelist as 'παραβολαι'. In the discussion which follows, therefore, I want to limit the term to the sense of a story or narrative, and I shall leave further discussions of parables until later, particularly until the examination of proverbial wisdom in chapter 6.

Jesus, it must be said, was a marvellous story-teller, and even his most familiar narratives we cannot choose but hear.

For his stories are weapons of controversy, his metaphors sharp and living. They meet a situation of conflict, whether between Jesus and the Pharisees or within our own hearts and consciences. Their language is distinctive and they *act* in their demand for an answer and their call for change. I hardly need elaborate on the dangers of treating these stories as allegory to be decoded image by image. Interpretations of the Good Samaritan by Origen or St. Augustine of Hippo are readily available in many standard commentaries, and it is not my intention to be drawn into a theological debate with them. As usual, I am more concerned with the text before us.

The challenge presented by a story like the Good Samaritan (Luke 10:30–7) is easy to perceive. There are characters with whom we can identify, and they act and interact in ways that should make us stop and think. Finally we are encouraged by the story to translate our reflection into action. 'Go and do as he did' (10:37). But some of Jesus' stories are much briefer and work upon us in quite a different way, not allowing us to interpret God's kingly rule into the conceivable terms of moral or social behaviour. Here is a good example:

> The kingdom of Heaven is like a treasure lying buried in a field. The man who found it, buried it again; and for sheer joy went and sold everything he had, and bought that field.
>
> (Matthew 13:44)

It is a perfect little story, with many of the hallmarks of Jesus' narrative technique: the man sold *everything*, his joy was unalloyed, the wording is crisp and precise. Its point, of course, lies beyond the narrative itself, for the delights of the buried treasure in the future are ensured by the activity of the man in the story, his finding, selling and buying.

Allow me here to comment on a simple, secular story with which we are all familiar, the story of the traffic lights. It has a beginning, as we wait at red. It has a middle as we move into gear on amber. It has an end as we travel forwards on green. But what sort of an end to the story is it? The end, in fact, is the beginning of our journey, a moving off on to the future road. The story has merely organised the time so that we can make a proper and purposeful beginning.

Now we can turn back to Jesus' story of the man with the buried treasure. The man, of course, is you and I. What Jesus is doing is organising us through a literary production. Like the traffic lights, he is putting us into a fiction, and if we are prepared to play according to the rules, we stand a better chance of getting our facts right. (You do not *have* to play the game of the traffic lights, but you will play the consequences if you do not!) The *literature* of Jesus' story in St. Matthew's Gospel is acting as a surrogate for Jesus' own *spoken* word. That spoken word was itself already standing in for the actions and emotions that it described. But that which is described, you may say, never actually happened; it was just a trace on a man's mind. So we go back in an infinite regression, and there is nothing absolutely there except the literature of the written word.

Yet we have already made our response to the art of that written word, felt its joy and its anticipation. We have responded to the text, but its infinitely regressive nature denies that it has any ultimate, final meaning. What we must do, then, is play its game in an ever lively anticipation of the apocalypse which its ending implies. There is no static vision in the stories of Jesus, but a road ahead, and unlike the road after the story of the traffic lights, it is mysterious and partakes of infinity.

AUTHOR, NARRATOR, CHARACTER AND READER

Jesus is the conscious author and narrator of his stories. But those two roles can sometimes be distinguished in the art of story-telling. The interaction of author, narrator, character and reader in our final experience of a narrative can be extremely complex and challenging. Consider the opening verses of the Revelation of John.

> This is the revelation given by God to Jesus Christ. It was given to him so that he might show his servants what must shortly happen. He made it known by sending his angel to his servant John, who, in telling all that he saw, has borne witness to the word of God and to the testimony of Jesus Christ.
>
> (Revelation 1:1–2)

The method of the narrative is triadic – from God, to Jesus Christ, to John. Throughout the book there is a subtle interplay between these three levels of narration. John bears witness to God and the testimony of Christ. The actual narrator, John himself, is very much a part of the narrative, not simply controlling it, but suffering fear and confusion (1:17), tears of distress (5:4), bitter distaste (10:10), astonishment (17:7), and a sense of inadequacy (19:10), as the action which he recounts plays upon him. And just as the author has set further levels beyond the immediate narrator, so too he draws his reader into his text by calling upon him to make judgements and an imaginative response. Alert readers will become aware that as the narrator is dramatically involved in the narrative, so they themselves play an active role as they may be deliberately led into misjudgement or guided towards conclusions which clearly require an exercise of self-criticism or moral reassessment.

Jesus, and the evangelists who shaped his stories into the written word, like a good novelist, are subtle indeed in the control of the reader, knowing that once the story is under way the reader will become inescapably involved in it, agonising with the hero in his tribulations and grinding his teeth against the machinations of his enemies. The good author knows exactly how far to keep readers in the dark, or what slant to put upon a particular scene in order to control their judgement. Sometimes an author is straightforward and reliable. Sometimes the author sets out to trick unwary readers, who, before they know what has happened, have compromised themselves and must change themselves and their judgements of who is good and who is bad. Come what may, the reader is there in the story as much as any of the characters. In the Bible, as in any other novel, we are all in the bloody book, and there is no better story-teller than Jesus Christ. His stories, and indeed the whole gospel narratives, not only say something but also do something. As we read, they force us to be involved, and to extend their images into our own experience of life. The story which they principally tell, like our lives, can be infinitely simple and yet profoundly mysterious.

THE STORY AS PROCLAMATION

Yet, when all is said and done, a story is told to be enjoyed, and I do not see why the story of the New Testament should be any different. After all, it has a happy ending, an assurance that all shall be well, and the writers who tell it are consummate artists. When we enjoy a book – I mean really enjoy it, not just for titillation or light amusement – we take what it says seriously and perhaps feel ourselves in the presence of one who knows something about human nature and the human predicament. Traditionally the good story-teller has been held in high respect, and still is today. And so, from all that I have said, it should be evident why I believe that the New Testament derives its authority not least from its narrative form, and that the telling of a story is a primary mode of religious proclamation. Moreover, the story told is not merely a form of address, but it acts upon us and causes change. The story not only 'says', it also 'does', and is therefore a proper form to proclaim the God who acts and who is known by what he has done. For, scripture says, 'the word of God is alive and active' (Hebrews 4:12).

We should be careful, therefore, about construing the New Testament as a collection of doctrines. We have seen how, from the earliest times, salvation history was not seen in terms of propositions, but in a recital of formative events like the Exodus or the Last Supper. Biblical doctrine, I suggest, was later inferred from this dramatic recital of the story, and indeed the narrative may be used to give authority to the proposals of theology. Thus the language of theology, concerning the doctrines of the Trinity, Christology, the Atonement, and so on, is second order and derived, while the language of the story is primary. This is not to underestimate the importance of Christian theology in the articulation of belief, but within any culture, theological proposals will be limited by the imaginative boundaries of the culture and its society. The lively, imaginative narratives of the New Testament are ever available to liberate the human imagination, so that by an imaginative act, Christian doctrine may become incarnate in our hearts and minds.

We have seen in this chapter that there is in the story a certain indeterminacy of meaning, and plural possibilities of interpretation in the subtle interplay of character and action, reader and narrator, character and reader. The reading of the gospel story of Jesus Christ living, crucified and risen, therefore, becomes a process which entails continuous revision and a continuous exercise of judgement. The subtlety that this requires is a good training for us as we encounter the depth and subtlety of the religious vision of the scriptures. For even as we delight in the artful imagination of the literature, we are brought to an awareness of the tremendous spiritual urgency that drives the writers of the New Testament.

The Time has come; the kingdom of God is upon you; repent and believe the Gospel.

(Mark 1:15)

We do not belong to night or darkness, and we must not sleep like the rest, but keep awake and sober.

(I Thessalonians 5:5–6)

The dramatic story of the New Testament is the last chapter in the great novel of the Bible. It had its beginning at the Creation and in the Garden of Eden, its middle in the Fall and the ensuing chaos, and now the hero has come to set things to rights. The best synopsis I know of the plot is in the opening lines of Milton's *Paradise Lost*:

> Of man's first disobedience, and the fruit
> Of that forbidden tree, whose mortal taste
> Brought death into the world, and all our woe
> With loss of Eden, till one greater Man
> Restore us, and regain the blissful seat,
> Sing, Heav'nly Muse . . .

We are in the last chapter, and the hidden author of the plot has ensured the outcome and guaranteed the shape of things to come. But, as in other stories, even at the end there is a duplicity between what is actually the case (in the divine order of things) and the perspective of we who are left with new assurance and hope. There is to the art symbol and surface, and it is in symbol that the truth is finally projected, in the hope of the Second Coming. Because of the story that has been told, we do not so much enter into new conditions of life, but everything that happens from now on has an entirely different meaning. We have read the final chapter of the novel, but there is always another chapter yet unwritten, and how that will end, we must wait and see.

5 Holding to the Tradition

Stand firm, then, brothers, and hold fast to the traditions which you have learned from us by word or by letter.

(II Thessalonians 2:15)

There are no simple answers to a question like, 'What is the gospel?', and usually our response will be directed by the formulations of creeds that were established long after the New Testament literature itself was written. From a reading of the New Testament, a fair answer may be that the gospel is the good news of Jesus Christ, who, through the transforming power of the Resurrection, is the way, the truth and the life. But if the answer implies that the transmission of that essential tradition is entrusted throughout the human race and from generation to generation, to the Church, then no doubt we have cause to be gloomy. For the Church itself often seems to be divided about the content of the tradition, and seems singularly unable to communicate the universal spirit of its claims to more than a small proportion of humanity.

Let us, then, go back to the beginnings in the New Testament. It did not take long for the primitive, first-hand experience of Jesus and the events of his ministry and Passion to be committed to writing, possible in the first instance in occasional letters written to meet a particular situation, such as Paul's letters to the Galatians or the Corinthians. Whether the *literary* history of the gospel began in this way, or in the formalities of liturgical worship, or simply as an aid to reflection, one thing is clear. Literature

59

selects, interprets and shapes experience. Literary representations of reality in no way correspond in every detail to the reality itself, so that the establishment of a tradition and holding to its essentials in the written word are difficult and elusive procedures.

TRADITION, PREACHING AND TEACHING

Paul's word for 'tradition' in II Thessalonians 2:15 is 'παράδοσις', which means literally a 'handing over'. In I Corinthians 11:12, he commends the Christians at Corinth for maintaining the παράδοσις which he had handed on to them. Included in this tradition is the account of the Last Supper which I discussed in the previous chapter (I Corinthians 11:23–6). But the *locus classicus* describing the Pauline tradition comes a little later in the same epistle.

> First and foremost, I handed on to you the facts which had been imparted to me: that Christ died for our sins, in accordance with the scriptures; that he was buried; that he was raised to life on the third day, according to the scriptures; and that he appeared to Cephas, and afterwards to the Twelve. Then he appeared to over five hundred of our brothers at once, most of whom are still alive, though some have died. Then he appeared to James, and afterwards to all the apostles.
>
> In the end he appeared even to me. It was like an abnormal birth; I had persecuted the church of God and am therefore inferior to all other apostles – indeed not fit to be called an apostle. However, by God's grace I am what I am, nor has his grace been given to me in vain; on the contrary, in my labours I have outdone them all – not I, indeed, but the grace of God working with me. But what matter, I or they? This is what we all proclaim, and this is what you believed.

(I Corinthians 15:3–11)

The inspired writer is a mouthpiece, proclaiming the gospel in a series of images drawn from experience and controlled by a fundamental faith in the mystery of divine creation and preservation. His is a poetic technique and a prophetic vocation.

Like poetry, the tradition plays upon the confused experience of life and death, selecting and shaping the portrait under the direction of an interpretation and within the ordinances of an authoritative literature – 'according to the scriptures'. The 'facts' of Christ are here limited to his death 'for our sins': his burial, his resurrection, and his post-resurrection appearances. Does this mean that the essence of the 'gospel' excludes the birth narratives, the accounts of Jesus' ministry, his disputes with the authorities, the promise of his second coming? Not necessarily, for as the gospel is proclaimed in a παράδοσις formed under a literary control, so it assumes the manifold interpretative complexity of an imaginative literature. For some, the perspective will emphasise Jesus' ministry of preaching and healing (St. Luke's Gospel). For others, Jesus is portrayed as the fulfilment of prophecy as Messiah (St.Matthew's Gospel). For yet others, the significance of the Incarnation focuses almost entirely upon the cross and the resurrection (St. Paul). Yet variety of interpretation does not imply a diversity of gospels. For there are other 'traditions' mentioned in the New Testament (e.g. Mark 7:13), which are entirely of human construction and which 'make God's word null and void'.

Before we continue with the literary exploration of the Christian tradition claimed by the canonical writers, I should briefly remind you of the familiar distinction between κήρυγμα (preaching) and διδαχή (teaching). Both Greek words, it should be said, overlap to a great extent with παράδοσις. Our concern in this chapter is primarily with κήρυγμα, the basic 'message' of the gospel which, according to Paul, 'did not sway you with subtle arguments; it carried conviction by spiritual power, so that your faith might be built not upon human wisdom but upon the power of God' (I Corinthians 2:4–5). The latter is the teaching, generally on morals and Church practice, sometimes on doctrine, which is drawn from the essential gospel tradition.

What, then, is the true gospel tradition to which St. Paul bids us hold fast? I have suggested in this book that the primary testimony of the New Testament is to the transforming power of the Resurrection, and that it is not enough to pursue a tradition that is formed by a dependence on the dry evidence of what can more or less be proved to have been the case. There is clearly a connection between our theological claims for the divinity of Jesus, the Trinity, the Atonement, and the other central doctrines of our faith, and the κήρυγμα of the New Testament, but it is not a simple or even very obvious connection. Questions about the 'real' Jesus and the 'real' gospel are liable very quickly to fall into an insoluble dualism: are we talking about the Jesus of History or the Christ of Faith? However far back we go to the primitive context, we always find it to be an interpretation, something not merely handed on but a tradition conveyed through the impressions and beliefs of those who have come to experience it in a variety of ways and under different circumstances. The danger point, it seems to me, is reached when the tradition begins to be seen not as intrinsically valuable, but as a means to some end, perhaps social control or moral justification. What the literature of the New Testament requires is precisely an unwavering attention to an artifact, the text, which unceasingly attracts us to the primitive context and catches us in a series of mutually enlightening interpretations as we endeavour to focus upon the heart of the matter. We hear the 'good news' in our stumbling attempts in the imaginative impressions of the New Testament writers.

As we have seen, the reader plays a part in the literary artificat, alongside author, narrator, character and action. He or she is an intrinsic part of the text, and therefore the tradition that is contained in the text remains intrinsically valuable. There is no outward projection of God who is then worshipped from afar and whose attributes are not really communicable to us in this life. The tradition which is an interpretation also involves us, so that, in Jesus' words in the Fourth Gospel, 'you will know that I am in my Father, and you in me and I in you' (John 14:20).

Religion which is a means to an end quickly becomes a tool to be manipulated for keeping other people in order. The New Testament literature, on the other hand, properly dispels any such objectification, and demands a pure attention to and involvement in the text, simply because it articulates in us (by the organising structures of story, poem, proverb and other literary forms) what is most important in human life and experience; a love which is quite unaccountable and mysterious. In the familiar words of the hymn:

> Then why, O blessèd Jesus Christ,
>   Should I not love thee well?
> Not for the sake of winning heaven,
>   Nor of escaping hell;
> Not from the hope of gaining aught
>   Not seeking a reward;
> But as thyself hast loved me,
>   O ever-loving Lord.

No doubt there is a fundamental *datum* of historical fact at the heart of the tradition; that Jesus, a Jew, was born in Roman Syria in the reign of the Emperor Augustus; that he was executed some thirty years later by the orders of the Judaean procurator, Pontius Pilate, under pressure from the Jews. Other people no doubt would wish to add to this basic minimum, but I would want to say that anything further demands interpretation. This may be under the shaping control of Old Testament prophecy, the sense of Jewish salvation history or *apocalyptic* – the literature which claims to reveal things normally hidden and to unveil the future. Now if, in their various ways, the New Testament writers identified and communicated Jesus under such a shaping control as one who perceived the world as the kingdom of a loving God, whom each one of us can know with intimate affection, and as one who ordered his life in terms of that perception, then I suggest that in them the tradition is truly preserved because they are, in different ways, individual and imaginative artists.

LITERATURE AND TRADITION

Many years ago T. S. Eliot aptly remarked in his essay 'Tradition and Individual Talent' that the blind and unyielding handing down of the ways of previous generations as 'tradition' should be positively discouraged. Tradition is something much richer than that, and requires of the artistic or poetic mind a historical sense which recognises that history is both past and present. Just as in the Passover or the Christian Eucharist, the recital of the story brings the power of the founding reality into the present, so the historical sense of the true traditionalist perceives the timeless in history and is fully aware of his own contemporary presence in the movement of time. Through this proper sense of the tradition we come to recognise that 'Jesus Christ is the same yesterday, today, and for ever' (Hebrews 13:8).

The recognition of this historical sense brings with it the realisation that no writer and no interpretation of the tradition is alone satisfactory or complete. Not only must each book of the New Testament be coherent within itself, but it must cohere with the whole order of the canon both as it developed in the early Christian centuries and as it reflects upon the earliest days of the church. As new layers are added to the tradition in the later books – the Fourth Gospel, perhaps, or I Peter – so the *entire* tradition is altered, earlier elements acting upon later and vice-versa. 'For Christ is like a single body with its many limbs and organs, which, many as they are, together make up one body' (I Corinthians 12:12).

Of course, the primary strands of the tradition are immensely important, and by them its true development must be judged. This judgement is a delicate balance of recognising valuable new insights and maintaining a proper conformity of these insights to what has gone before. The true development will enhance and illuminate the earlier expression of the tradition. Real originality is not quirky or self-indulgent. It is aware of itself as part of a living stream, a development wherein the true original in the present is aware of the past in a way in which perhaps the past was not aware of itself. It is not that the later writers simply know more, but that the tradition feeds them from a past which is infinitely rich and rare. 'You have been born anew, not of mortal parentage but of immortal, through the living and enduring word of God' (I Peter 1:23).

Nor, finally, is this to suggest that holding to the tradition requires an immense learning in what has gone before. What I am suggesting is that the tradition to which the apostolic writers appealed demanded a great exercise of the imagination together with an unfailing readiness to be conscious of the past and surrender oneself to it. It is both a loss of oneself in what has gone before and an imaginative proclamation of the tradition thus absorbed in terms accessible to the present. In the hands of the evangelist and apostle, then, the tradition of the gospel may become all things to all people. So writes St. Paul:

To Jews I became like a Jew to win Jews . . . To win Gentiles, who are outside the Law, I made myself like one of them . . . To the weak I became weak, to win the weak. Indeed, I have become everything in turn to men of every sort, so that in one way or another I may save some. All this I do for the sake of the Gospel, to bear my part in proclaiming it.

(I Corinthians 9:20–3)

THE PROBLEM OF THE SECOND COMING

To argue for the coherence of the New Testament canon is not to deny that there are apparent inconsistencies in its writings. Certainly there are literary disagreements, for example, between the three synoptic gospels, which may be attributed to the way in which they use Old Testament material, or perhaps to the way in which one writer reshaped the material and style of another. Literary variations may be the result of early theological movement. But I want to dwell for a moment upon one important problem for the apostolic writers – the increasing delay of the expected *Parousia*, the future return of Christ in glory to judge the living and the dead, and to terminate the present world order.

The expectation of a speedy second coming seems deeply rooted in early Christian belief. In his first letter to the Thessalonians, Paul wrote that 'we who are left alive until the Lord comes shall not forestall those who have died' (4:15). No doubt, the same expectation is expressed in a much later writing, I John: 'My children, this is the last hour!' (2:18). But generally the delay of the Parousia brought about a change in the nature of the Christian hope. In his later writings, Paul seems to have ceased to expect that he would be still alive when it took place (Philippians 1:20ff), and the new form of the hope is shaped by literary means. To start with it was reconstructed from the resources of Jewish *apocalyptic literature*, which, among other things was tailor-made to comfort a people suffering persecution, since the ancient apocalypses foretold that the end of all things would be preceded by a time of confusion and anarchy. An early example of the genre, the Book of Daniel, was probably written during the persecution of Antiochus Epiphanes (175–163 BC), to comfort the Jewish people and assure them of the coming Divine intervention.

> . . . and I saw one like a man coming with the clouds of heaven; he approached the Ancient in Years and was

presented to him. Sovereignty and glory and kingly power were given to him, so that all peoples and nations of every language should serve him; his sovereignty was to be an everlasting sovereignty which should not pass away, and his kingly power such as should never be impaired.

(Daniel 7:13–14)

In the New Testament, the time of suffering which is to precede the Parousia is sanctified by a comparison with the sufferings of Christ before his triumph (I Peter 4:12–13). The apocalyptic descriptions of tribulation and the 'great Day' in 2 Thessalonians 1:6–10 are most un-Pauline in their expression, and I suspect they are something of an afterthought drawn almost directly from a contemporary apocalypse. Apart from the identification of the Messianic figure from heaven with Jesus Christ, they are not essentially Christian, rather an accretion to the tradition. Finally, the most familiar of such passages in the New Testament outside the Revelation of John itself, the so-called 'Little Apocalypse' of Mark 13, follows closely the procedures of Daniel, not only in its imagery ('they will see they Son of Man coming in the clouds with great power and glory' – 13:26), but in its linking of mythical description with contemporary events. I have no doubt that this chapter should be read in the context of the political and military upheavals of the late fifties and early sixties A.D., and that their traumatic effect produced a literature whose imaginative insight and self-consistency ranges far beyond the local events of their origin.

But what, in the end, is the effect of this adoption of a literary genre in order to come to terms with the practical problem of the delay of the Parousia? The mythical accretion, it seems to me, had the wholly beneficial effect of purifying the tradition of local history and of the false hope of a literal early return of the Lord. It enabled the apostolic writers to grasp more adequately the central concerns of the gospel. For, in Christ, the restoration of all things has ceased to be a possibility, because it already *is*, being grounded in the once-and-for-all act of salvation. The vision of the end is simply the fulfilment of what has already been realised, and the tradition links the Parousia inextricably with the earthly events of the life and death of Jesus.

> Have you forgotten that when we were baptised into union with Christ Jesus we were baptised into his death? By baptism we were buried with him, and lay dead, in order that, as Christ was raised from the dead, so also we might set our feet upon the new path of life.

> (Romans 6:3–4)

The whole force and imagery of the descriptions of Jesus' life and ministry in the Fourth Gospel derive from the shape and significance of the Passion, which is finally drawn to a climax in the great cry from the cross, 'τετέλεσται' ('It is accomplished'). The death of Christ is the end and fulfilment of all things, a conclusion and the glorious realisation of the kingdom of which literature had given expression.

A brief illustration from secular writing of how literature can rescue an eternal truth that is in danger of being lost in the pedantic toils of historical literalism is W. B. Yeats's poem 'Sailing to Byzantium'. At least it might dispel any silly notions that to expect the Lord literally to appear on the clouds of heaven next week or next year is true to the tradition of primitive Christianity:

> O Sages standing in God's holy fire
> As in the gold mosaic of a wall,
> Come from the holy fire, perne in a gyre,
> And be the singing-masters of my soul.
> Consume my heart away; sick with desire
> And fastened to a dying animal
> It knows not what it is; and gather me
> Into the artifice of eternity.

Once out of nature I shall never take
My bodily form from any natural thing,
But such a form as Grecian goldsmiths make
Of hammered gold and gold enamelling
To keep a drowsy Emperor awake;
Or set upon a golden bough to sing
To lords and ladies of Byzantium
Of what is past, or passing or to come.

I do not pretend that the poem is Christian, nor do I offer any detailed commentary on it. But it does make my point as a piece of literature, alongside the literature of the New Testament. The bird sings of yesterday, today and what is to come, of the past, the passing and the coming (compare Hebrews 13:8). It is a mythical creature, 'out of nature', drawn by art out of life in order to give shape to life in the perspective of time. This shape is described as 'the artifice of eternity', related to the dying animals that we are. Art is the important expression of life's need to have a form of belonging, to exist in the context of a beginning and an end. Thus, a gospel reading for Christmas Day opens with the words, 'In the beginning' (John 1:1), while a reading for Easter Day concludes, 'I am the first and the last' (Revelation 1:18).

WORSHIP AND THE TRADITION

I refer to our *liturgical* use of the New Testament tradition in contemporary worship, because I believe that that is one of the primary ways in which we hold to the tradition, and that the literary shape of much scripture is derived from the eternal concerns of the worship of a God who is the creator and preserver of all things. There is a strong argument, for example, for seeing the structure of St. Matthew's Gospel as formed upon the shape of the Jewish Festal Year with its three pilgrim-feasts of Passover, Pentecost and Tabernacles.

The sense which we maintain in our liturgical year from advent to advent, of the rhythms of eternity in history, is deeply rooted in the apostolic tradition.

More particularly the formal cadences of worship can be heard in the narratives and preaching of the very earliest Christian writings. I have already referred to Paul's account of the Last Supper in I Corinthians 11:23–6. The formality of these verses, together with their parallels in the synoptic gospels, make it very likely that they are drawn from an already established practice of eucharistic worship. Then there are numerous passages which conform to the pattern of hymn or prayer, often in a typically Jewish way: the three great canticles of St. Luke's Gospel, put into the mouths of characters in the narratives, and still used daily – the Magnificat (1:46–55), the Benedictus (1:67–79), and the Nunc Dimittis (2:29–32); the songs of the Revelation of John (7:12, 11:15, 19:6–8); the Lord's Prayer itself (Matthew 6:9–13, Luke 11:2–4); and numerous other fragments (Acts 4:24–6, Colossians 1:15–20, Ephesians 5:14). I have offered only a small selection, and it is possible to debate their origins in worship. But I would argue that their formality, and frequently their rhythmic and symmetrical nature, not only often lead us back into Jewish worship, but are typical of the way in which a tradition discovers and preserves itself as its primary materials and experiences are explored and articulated in a literary recollection in tranquillity. At a slightly later stage, διδαχή develops from κήρυγμα, as possibly in the case of I Peter as a sermon recalling the faithful to their baptismal promises. No doubt the early tradition and worship provided the grounds for the development of secondary reflections upon ethics and manners.

LANGUAGE AS RE-ENACTMENT

I conclude this chapter with a statement of my belief in language as the re-enactment of the primitive experience. I see the diverse strands of the New Testament as a rhetorical strategy to preserve the tradition of Christian belief in the impersonal artistry of literary forms. Diversity there may be, but there is no room for the radical idiosyncrasies of an individual or a lunatic fringe. My underlying conviction is that the apostolic gospel is essentially not a complex affair. There are in scripture commonly recognised norms of confession; a belief in the life and death of Jesus of Nazareth and the acknowledgement of his resurrection as the decisive moment in salvation history as it is drawn from the Old Testament.

But while the essential contemplation of God through Jesus is restrained by the art of the apostolic κήρυγμα, Christian theology begins its task of communicating with a complex and diverse environment, its inner consistency ruled by the primitive standards. Doctrinal development continues as culture and society itself changes, and new controversies are thrown up. If my claims for the art of the traditional literature have tended to make it seem rather hard and unyielding, then I must emphasise that the Christian faith has never rested just upon information about Jesus, but upon witness to him. That witness, as we have it in the New Testament, combines a remarkable variety with uniformity. There is no line to be drawn between knowledge of Jesus and early response to him in the written word, and therein lies the subtlety of our faith.

6 Proverbial Wisdom

PROVERB AND APHORISM

It is not altogether surprising that an *aphoristic* mode of writing has become increasingly apparent in modern literature. In the seventeenth century, Pascal suggested that his 'disordered' form of discourse was the only proper way to claim a 'true order' in our fallen world. All the more appropriately in our own confused and fragmented century, this broken and often paradoxical style is employed in a wide range of literature, in fiction (Kafka and Jorge Luis Borges), in philosophy (Wittgenstein), and in theology (Martin Buber). Its characteristics are an ambiguity which does not strive for conceptual precision; a fragmentariness which does not necessarily seek to sum up life in one overarching view; and an effect of disorientation which breaks up any coherent vision of life yet implies an ultimate reorientation through a radical change of values. The aphoristic mode of writing occurs also in the gospels:

Love your enemies.

(Matthew 5:44)

How blest you are when men hate you.

(Luke 7:22)

Whoever cares for his own safety is lost; but if a man will let himself be lost for my sake and for the Gospel, that man is safe.

(Mark 8:35)

The aphorism, I suggest, is a growing point of prose, a radical reinterpretation and enlivening of what is old in tradition.

We have seen something of how 'narrative theology' has recently become so popular. It has had the beneficial effect of helping to restore the sense of wholeness and the literary integrity of the biblical texts. But it has also tended to divert attention away from other literary forms, apart from the story and narrative, and the different role that these can play in the literary structures of the New Testament. With the *proverb* or *aphorism* we return to the Hebrew notion of *mašal* (see also above, p.52). I suspect that its root meaning is close to our idea of a riddle, but it comes to embrace many forms of figurative saying, from a simple comparison or simile to an extended and complex narrative. Its development in the proverbial wisdom of the Old Testament and the Apocrypha (Proverbs, Ecclesiastes, Wisdom of Solomon, Ecclesiasticus) is well documented, and I have listed one or two of the major critical works in my Reading List. But the aphoristic literature of the New Testament has been granted less attention, even though it lies at the heart of Jesus' ministry as it is recorded in the gospels.

I have referred to the terms *proverb* and *aphorism*. There is a difference between them, although I would not wish to distinguish them too sharply. Generally, a proverb is a pithy saying derived from common use and with a popular origin. Perhaps St. Matthew's, 'Each day has troubles enough of its own' (6:34) would be a good example. We certainly now readily use it proverbially. An aphorism, on the other hand, as a principle or precept expressed briefly, implies a more literary origin in a specific author or source. It might be applied to those gospel sayings which seem to originate from an individual mind and a particular situation:

> Foxes have their holes, the birds their roosts; but the Son of Man has nowhere to lay his head.

> (Matthew 8:20)

But perhaps what they have in common is more significant than their differences. They are metaphorical in their language. They do not employ the techniques of narrative, but expose a tension between the general and the particular, the principle and its application in a particular case. They are provocative and challenging through paradox, and sometimes irony. Above all, like the *mašal*, they are rooted in a tradition and traditional knowledge, and work to the discovery and maintenance of that living tradition. Thus, in St. Matthew's Gospel, Jesus emphasises that his task is to fulfil and complete the Old Testament tradition, and he prefaces the paradoxical and radical assessment of the Law in the Sermon on the Mount with this assurance:

> Do not suppose that I have come to abolish the Law and the prophets; I did not come to abolish, but to complete.

> (Matthew 5:17)

Having mentioned these characteristics of the proverb and the aphorism, and before we take our discussion any further, I suggest that we refer to a comment on metaphorical language by one of the most perceptive of English literary critics, the poet S.T. Coleridge in his 'sermon' *The Statesman's Manual*.

> It is among the miseries of the present age that it recognizes no medium between *Literal* and *Metaphorical* . . . a Symbol. . . is characterized by a translucence of the

Special in the Individual or of the General in the Especial or of the Universal in the General. Above all by the translucence of the Eternal through and in the Temporal.

This description of metaphorical and symbolic language provides an illuminating commentary upon Jesus' aphoristic teaching in the synoptic gospels. At the heart of it is the individual as a member of a community. This individual is repeatedly viewed in relation to the whole of humanity or earthly life, or, most often, to God. The particular is seen in the context of the universal. The radical nature of the teaching frequently rests upon the contrast between the individual's anxiety to preserve one's own life and the giving all to God's care. This *mašal* in St. Luke's Gospel has its parallel in St. Matthew:

> 'Therefore,' he said to his disciples, 'I bid you put away anxious thoughts about food to keep you alive and clothes to cover your body. Life is more than food, the body more than clothes.'

> (Luke 12:22–3)

Prudent care is, of course, necessary. We might recall the parable of the house built on the rock (Luke 6:48–9). But anxiety which lies outside a commitment to the kingdom of God is self-defeating. We cannot be the slave of two masters (Matthew 6:24), yet even under God's care we must be watchful in a threatening world; 'be wary as serpents, innocent as doves' (Matthew 10:16).

THE INDIVIDUAL AND THE UNIVERSAL

Jesus and his teaching embody the proverbial tension between the individual and the universal. His is a new kind of teaching, for 'he speaks with *authority*' (Mark 1:27). Many of his sayings are drawn from ancient proverbial wisdom (Matthew 24:28, Luke 7:35, 10:3). His authority often claims to rest upon the true and unperverted traditions of the Jews (Mark 7:9). Yet while he cannot be understood apart from the law and the prophets, Jesus remains the individual whose wisdom expresses a discontinuity which is yet continuous with the divine order. He disorientates in order to reorientate. In his lack of one overarching view that embraces the multitude of life's situations, his emphasis on individual experience, and his sense of God's care for human ψυχή (life), Jesus contrasts with the prudential wisdom of Proverbs.

> Idle hands make a man poor;
> busy hands grow rich.
> A thoughtful son puts by in summer;
> a son who sleeps at harvest in disgrace.

> (Proverbs 10:4–5)

Jesus' wisdom replaces this counsel of security with an alternative emphasis on the experience of life under God. (Only Ecclesiastes in the Old Testament proposes a similar sense of individual experience and the temporary nature of human concerns.)

The tension between the individual and the universal in the proverbs and aphorisms of the gospels is also a tension between a piercing human wisdom, which we might call common sense, and traditional scriptural wisdom. They place the tradition in a wholly human context, and this dialectic employs the obliqueness and inherent inadequacy of metaphorical language to shift the focus of Jesus' authority beyond the practical securities of human affairs to the elusive, eternal concerns of the divine rule. One of the most familiar sayings of the New Testament illustrates well the strained language of a metaphor whose very inadequacy makes an extreme point. It is oblique with a sense of humour drawn from the midst of everyday life.

> It is easier for a camel to pass through the eye of a needle than for a rich man to enter the kingdom of God.

(Mark 10:25)

Similar incongruities which border on the comic can be found in Luke 6:39, 41, and Matthew 23:24.

At the beginning of this chapter I distinguished the aphorisms and proverbs of the New Testament from the narrative forms which now receive so much critical attention. Yet they also have much in common with those forms. In chapter 2 I pointed out that a story develops in an essentially contingent way and not by a logical sequence of cause and effect. Its incidents are contingent and its nature is *teleological* – the development is determined not causally but by a final purpose or design. Similarly, the paradoxical wisdom of the proverbial teaching reverses the natural expectations of cause and effect, and directs us towards a future hope. It abandons precise causal connections in favour of juxtaposition and extension.

> . . . among you, whoever wants to be great must be your servant, and whoever wants to be first must be the willing slave of all. For even the Son of Man did not come to be served but to serve, and to give up his life as a ransom for many.

(Mark 10:43–5)

The passage begins with two parallel sayings, the second being an intensification of the first: great/first, servant/slave of all. These are then applied to the particular case of the Son of Man, and finally extended to embrace the ultimate and universal purpose of his servanthood.

From all that I have said of the proverbial wisdom of the gospels, it should be clear that its teaching is not primarily concerned with the motives or rightness of moral behaviour. Even while the Sermon on the Mount claims not to abolish but to complete the Law, the demands of this teaching are not simply for conduct in accordance with fixed precepts. Nor does it suggest a painstaking scrutiny of reasons for particular action. Rather, it is a call that all our endeavours are to be seen and judged within the new experience of God in Christ Jesus. The individual now must live his or her life under the acceptance of God's care and sovereignty, and this calls for spontaneity, a creative sense of adventure under divine inspiration, and an ultimate faith which is prepared to live a life of vision outside the mechanical operation of rules and legislation. The literary tensions that express this ascendancy of the paradoxical and gracious images of the Kingdom over the anxious and self-defeating arguments of men, is well expressed in Jesus' reply to those who accuse him of casting out devils by Beelzebub:

> If it is by Beelzebub that I cast out devils, by whom do your own people drive them out? If this is your argument, they themselves will refute you. But if it is by the finger of God that I drive out the devils, then be sure the kingdom of God has already come upon you.

> (Luke 11:19–20)

THE POETRY OF THE PROVERB

The proverbial wisdom that is the subject of this chapter is a form of poetic expression. More common in the Ancient Near East than in our own culture, except perhaps in the specialised literary sense to which I have referred, proverbs and aphorisms in the New Testament have a sharpness and brilliance which demands a high degree of intellectual activity. So far I have spoken rather generally of their purpose and effect. A word now is needed on the literary techniques that underlie this brilliance.

The paradoxes of Jesus' remarks are often antithetical in form.

> Whoever seeks to save his life will lose it; and whoever loses it will save it, and live.

> (Luke 17:33)

The antitheses here set up are expressed as a *chiasmus*, inverting in the second sentence the order of the first. We can write it in this way:

This is a common device in the gospels (Mark 2:27, Matthew 10:16, Luke 16:13, etc.) In each case there is a deliberate confusion of linguistic order (see above, p. 40), a breaking of the mould, which changes values and effects a radically new vision. The words themselves are made to take on an entirely new meaning.

This antithetical device undoubtedly derives from that most basic form of poetic expression in Hebrew literature, *parallelismus membrorum*, of which a good example is Mark 10:43–5, quoted just above. The reduplication that occurs in these parallel sayings is not simply restatement (*tautology*), nor is it designed to sharpen the profile of a statement or concept. Rather, it pulls the language out, stretching it so that it takes on an edge which points beyond the original statement. Such a saying is properly an aphorism as I have defined it above, for it is the product of a particular intellectual and literary exercise. Technically it is known as *synthetic parallelism*, in which the second statement develops or intensifies the first. There are two other forms of parallelism. In the *synonymous* form, both statements say practically the same thing. This is common in the proverbs of the Old Testament, but its static quality has little place in the gospels. *Antithetic parallelism* is common in the chiastic sayings that I have just considered.

Both synthetic and antithetic parallelism are characteristic of a New Testament proverbial wisdom that is open and points beyond itself, linking the particular and the individual to the eternal and the infinite. The interpretation of these sayings is never simple or restricted, for they are based in the teeming experience of life and their stretching of language demands a keen intellectual response of the reader. This intellectual exercise consists in a conforming of the language and its vision to the events and experience which originally gave it utterance. We know what it is to love our friends and hate our enemies. But how do we return to that experience in the way Jesus exhorts, and keep the language within recognisable limits of meaning? Or again, dare we humble ourselves to see if the promised exaltation is consonant with our understanding of the word 'exalt'?

Here is a challenge indeed! In these sayings there is a radical dislocation of language which, quite literally, takes on new life and suggests a new order and hope for human experience. Coming to terms with such proverbial wisdom is an intellectual, moral and spiritual exercise on the pattern of St. Paul's great description of resurrection. The advent of new life involves a death, a radical abandonment of old categories in the hope of what is promised.

> So it is with the resurrection of the dead. What is sown in the earth as a perishable thing is raised imperishable. Sown in humiliation, it is raised in glory; sown in weakness, it is raised in power; sown as an animal body, it is raised as a spiritual body.
>
> (I Corinthians 15:42–4)

Thus the language of the proverbs and aphorisms of the

gospels, in its initial fragmentariness and its effect of disorientation which points towards a greater coherence, partakes of the testimony of the scriptures to the transforming power of the Resurrection. It recognises the manifold character of experience in its refusal to be trapped in one interpretation, or fixed in one sense. Yet, with all its confusion of language levels and its subversion of the meaning of words, proverbial wisdom in the New Testament affirms an ultimate order in the promised kingdom of God, realised already in the life, death and resurrection of Jesus Christ. Therefore I conclude a chapter about a literary form which is, by nature, exhortatory and open to the future, with a simple statement of the condition to which the proverb and aphorism point:

> There is one body and one Spirit, as there is also one hope held out in God's call to you; one Lord, one faith, one baptism; one God and Father of all, who is over all and through all and in all.
>
> (Ephesians 4:4–6)

7 Fictions and Fantasy

ORDER AND DISORDER

In his first letter to the Corinthians, Paul warns that in the experience and inspiration of Christian worship there must always be an exercise of judgement and controlled interpretation:

> when you meet for worship, each of you contributes a hymn, some instruction, a revelation, an ecstatic utterance, or the interpretation of such an utterance. All of these must aim at one thing: to build up the church. If it is a matter of ecstatic utterance, only two should speak, or at most three, one at a time, and someone must interpret. If there is no interpreter, the speaker had better not address the meeting at all, but speak to himself and to God. Of the prophets, two or three may speak, while the rest exercise their judgement upon what is said. If someone else, sitting in his place, receives a revelation, let the first speaker stop. You can all prophesy, one at a time, so that the whole congregation may receive instruction and encouragement. It is for prophets to control prophetic inspiration, for the God who inspires them is not a God of disorder but of peace.
>
> (I Corinthians 14:26–33)

Paul certainly does not deny a place in worship to spontaneity and ecstacy. But inspiration and revelation must be steadied by reasonable interpretation and a proper sense of order. Everything must be constructive, contributing to the building up of church life. Elsewhere in the letters to the Corinthians, in Ephesians 2:20–2, and in I Peter 2:4–6, the image of the Church as the temple building underlines the sense of community in which right judgement and order are the foundation of stability and harmony. The opposite of such stability is indicated by the word 'disorder', which Paul uses in I Corinthians 14:33. In Greek it means instability or the lack of a fixed point, and is contrasted with the idea of peace.

This sense of instability comes close to the heart of early usages in English of the word 'fantasye' which shares its Greek origins with our word 'fancy'. In the fourteenth-century writings of Geoffrey Chaucer it means a mental image of something that does not exist. It can be a delightful image, but the tone usually implies hallucination, delusion and the unstable wanderings of wishful thinking. Later on, Shakespeare in *Romeo and Juliet* writes of dreams

> Which are the children of an idle brain,
> Begot of nothing but vain fantasy;
> Which is as thin of substance as the air,
> And more inconstant than the wind.

Again, there is the sense of wavering instability in the inconstancy of the wind. Finally, at the end of the seventeenth century, John Bunyan wrote the words of the familiar hymn in *The Pilgrim's Progress*:

> Hobgoblin nor foul Fiend
> Can daunt his spirit;
> He knows he at the end
> Shall Life inherit.
> Then Fancies flee away,
> He'll fear not what men say,
> He'll labour night and day
> To be a Pilgrim.

But I would not wish to confuse 'fantasy' or 'fancy' with the faculty of the imagination. In chapter 3 I mentioned that for Samuel Taylor Coleridge, writing early in the nineteenth century, the imagination was the supreme gift of the poet, nothing less than the reflection in him of the divine act of creation. In contrast, fancy is the haunt of jumbled memories and dreams, a mad riot of images that have slipped out of the order of time and space.

However, while literary criticism may distinguish between these terms, in the practice of art, literature and religious belief the distinction is not always an easy one. In his second letter to the Thessalonians, Paul writes that God puts 'those doomed to destruction . . . under a *delusion*, which works upon them to believe the lie' (2:10–11). His word for 'delusion' implies a *wandering* from the path of truth, suggesting the fantastic and insubstantial vagaries of a fantasy world.

In the letter of Jude, the author writes of ungodly perverters of the faith whose 'dreams lead them to defile the body, to flout authority, and to insult celestial beings' (verse 8). The supernatural information supplied in such dreams is vain and infamous, in contrast with the supernatural words of the archangel Michael (verse 9). But while the gross immorality of the wicked men who are described in this letter marks them out for ruin, where in the end do we distinguish between the wild imaginings of fantasy and the creative genius of the imagination? Take, for example, this passage from St. Matthew's Gospel:

Jesus again gave a loud cry, and breathed his last. At that moment the curtain of the temple was torn in two from top to bottom. There was an earthquake, the rocks split and the graves opened, and many of God's saints were raised from sleep; and coming out of their graves after his resurrection they entered the Holy City, where many saw them.

(Matthew 27:50–3)

Taken literally, I simply do not believe that account, any more than I condone the activities of the dreamers of the letter of Jude. I can readily understand how someone outside the Christian tradition might find it difficult to assimilate a narrative which speaks of dead men rising from the tombs, accompanied by earthquakes and tremors; or at least, to assimilate it as the factual record which it apparently purports to be. But here we are back with the subject of chapter 2, the problem of the sense of history. Now if we take Matthew's account of the crucifixion as *imaginative fiction*, in what sense is it different from the vain delusions of dream and fantasy and how might it be described as true?

IMAGINATION AND ESCAPISM

There certainly is a difference between escapist, fantasy literature and imaginative literature. In the first category I would include pornography, sado-masochistic writings, most science fiction and sentimental 'romances'. In the second category there would be Aeschylus, Dante, Shakespeare and, in a unique way, much of the New Testament. The nineteenth-century American critic James Russell Lowell made a forthright attack on the 'misunderstanding' caused by the confusion of 'imagination' with 'mere fantasy, the image-making power common to all who have the gift of dreams'. I hope that I have made the distinction between them clear. I should now say that I believe there may be blurred edges, and we should look at how this blurring might affect the New Testament and its interpretation. Is the Revelation of John the work of an imaginative and inspired genius, or simply a product of fantasy? And why are some fictional reconstructions of the life of Jesus Christ, even though written with sincerity and devotion, to be consigned to the literature of fantasy as they entirely miss any actual encounter with the living Christ? We must explore how they are different from the imaginative fiction of St. Matthew's Gospel.

Let us start by considering the nature of *facts* in imaginative fictions, from a literary rather than from an historical point of view. We might say that the task of interpretation depends upon the facts of the case; interpreters are drawn together in the commonwealth of the facts. But as we recall the problem of the hermeneutic circle (see p. 42 above), we are bound to ask whether there is much in the way of fact in any given text which is not determined by the perspective of readers who, consciously or unconsciously, interpret as they read. Take, for example, the sentence: 'At that moment, the curtain of the temple was torn in two from top to bottom.' Whether or not that was actually the case at the moment of Jesus' death, most Christian interpreters are content to understand it symbolically in the sense that by his death Jesus has opened a new access to God for his people. In the Jewish tradition, only a specially chosen priest could enter the sanctuary and see the curtain before the Holy of Holies (Luke 1:9). Now, in Christ, a 'new, living way' is open to all (Hebrews 10:20). Thus, a *figurative* interpretation of this passage in the Gospel has actually suggested the image of the torn curtain.

Two things should be borne in mind here. First, it is dangerous to rule out any interpretation by appealing to facts if interpretation is itself creative of the facts. Second, our reading of the incident of the torn curtain depends ultimately on agreement and on shared beliefs and assumptions. To those who are outside the Judaeo-Christian tradition of the temple and its worship, it may seem either unlikely or of academic interest.

For the Christian there are many constraints upon the interpretation of a scriptural text, not least the institutional constraints of the Church. I suspect, for example, that whether or not you subscribe to the notion of episcopacy ultimately determines, in fact, how you read the New Testament, rather than vice-versa. Also, the root of many existing disagreements between Christians and churches is simply a lack of suitable facts in the scriptures upon which interpretations can agree. Most of us are trapped too tightly in our own hermeneutic circle of assumption–text–revised assumption.

The way out, I believe, is not by an historical method of attempting to prove or establish the 'facts of the case', for, as I have already suggested, the New Testament tends to frustrate the categories and criteria of the historian. It is, initially at least, by literary means – by an imaginative openness which breaks through the self-engrossed spiral of the hermeneutic circle and reaches out to the hearts and minds of those who stand outside.

In the first place we must be prepared to dispense with the simple division of subject and object which still haunts so much of our thinking. It would be so easy to separate 'me' from all the objects around me, so that knowledge became clear-cut and the text of the New Testament equally and in the same way available to me and to you. But that is a fantasy, for it is never possible to separate the observer from the observed since in our observations we continually see ourselves in our confused vision. As St. Paul wrote, 'Now we see only puzzling reflections in a mirror, but then we shall see face to face' (I Corinthians 13:12).

Thus, to read the New Testament is, as much as anything, to grow in self-knowledge, and the rich variety of what is 'out there' in the world and in the divine mystery is revealed in the active imaginations of readers who are continually aware of their own role in the drama they witness. As they are excluded from the world of fantasy, they play their full part in the drama of the imagination. In this dramatic role, the human being is not simply a child of nature and history, but also a child of language and conditioned by it. Language is fundamental, even beyond the sense of history. 'When all things began, the Word already was' (John 1:1). *Literature* finds its genesis in poetry which, at its purest, makes little distinction between figurative and literal language (see p. 28

above), and its metaphors draw together in the processes of interpretation the self and that which is beyond the self and perhaps, literally, beyond language itself. In the Old Testament, Job finally meets his God in silence (Job 40:3–5, 42:5–6), while in Psalm 19, the heavens, night and day glorify God, 'and this without speech or language' (verse 3). But the point is that these images are rendered *in* language, metaphors by which that which is beyond language is conveyed.

In his poetry, man who is the child of language employs words to realise the powerful visions of the imagination. These visions create a mythology that is cast in the metaphorical language of poetry and literature. I should add here that I believe that *mythology*, as I have already suggested in chapter 2, despite its associations with legend and even fantasy, has been a major literary influence in fostering the growth of historical narrative and a sense of history. Furthermore, the metaphorical and mythological nature of the New Testament writings cannot be separated from their role as κήρυγμα, which is the vehicle of what is traditionally called revelation.

If all this seems rather elusive and theoretical, let me now try and relate the imaginative fictions of the gospels to some modern fictional attempts to re-tell the same story. The gospels, then, are literature with a specific kerygmatic purpose. Yet they share with many other literary narratives an unwillingness to approach a subject head-on, and they have a deviousness and elusiveness which matches well the enigma of the gospel itself. Indeed, we often find that direct communication of the gospel can easily become too self-conscious, propagandist and platitudinous, and thus degenerate into the perversions of the abstraction and the meaningless catch-phrase. The true witness is unself-conscious or, perhaps ironically, self-effacing, in literature not so much simply an intellectual stimulant as prompting in the reader a free response of imagination, thought and emotion.

A glance at the approach to Jesus Christ by modern

novelists sheds light on the oblique literary nature of the gospels. There are those, like Lloyd Douglas in *The Robe* and the Jewish author Max Brod in *The Master*, who have tried to update the gospels, implying that they are, fundamentally, biographical chronicles and producing works whose very historical brilliance is an obstruction to an encounter with Jesus Christ. Their historicism leads them into the realms of fantasy. Other novelists have been truer to the gospels, making no attempt to provide an historical image of Jesus. They begin rather with the experience of the contemporary world. Jesus stands behind the dramas of their novels, not directly, but reflected in character and patterning. In Dostoevsky's *The Idiot* or Nikos Kazantzakis' *Christ Recrucified*, for example, the essential pattern of the gospel narratives is shown to be essential to the life of humanity. Such novels, it seems to me, understand the nature and function of myth in culture and society better than the 'historical fiction' of Douglas and Brod. In fact the flat, literal quality of most historical novels is probably as as good an example of the dangers of *demythologising* as you will find. In them Jesus becomes simply a remote historical figure with little bearing upon our present experience.

Christ Recrucified is far more aware of the concrete, reserved and symbolic nature of the gospels than is *The Robe*. For the gospels, like Kazantzakis, work by indirection, concerned with Jesus, not so much as an historical figure as one imaginatively at the centre of human life endured to its very depths. What the gospels do not say is as important as what they do say, and that their perspectives should be Christian is more important than that they should make overt claims to be such. Why, for example, does St. Mark's Gospel (assuming that it ends properly at 16:8) not press home the *fact* of the resurrection? Perhaps, I suggest, the resurrection is a truth of the imagination, implicit in this Gospel from the very start for those who have eyes to perceive it. In one of his sermons, the theologian Austin Farrer actually puts words into the mouth of the evangelist:

How shall I make you see the resurrection? he replied. I show you, in all my book, the kingship of God present in the action of a man.

Or perhaps it was simply that he knew that very often in literature what is not written is more important than what is. Such incompleteness and hiddenness, indeed such secrecy which requires of the reader an enormous exercise of the imagination, indicates that God is far greater than anything that is capable of direct, literal expression. And it is in the nature of a story to end at the beginning of a new story, looking forward in hope. In the end, the new story is the important one, and it has always been there, hidden in the story that is told, a proclamation in riddles, a salvation though only in hope (Romans 8:24).

THE IMAGINATION AS THREAT AND AS A CREATIVE FORCE

It is partly our long obsession with the historicity of the New Testament that has led us to feel uneasy with it as myth, art or literature. But not entirely. From the early days of the Jewish religion, figurative art was seen as a threat. 'You shall not make a carved image for yourself', runs the second commandment (Exodus 20:4, Deuteronomy 5:8). Among certain Christian groups the fury of iconoclasm, particularly in later times, has been mainly directed against the images of visual art, but the distrust of the literary language and imagery of the scriptures has been far more widespread and far more insidious. Imagination has always been regarded as a dangerous tool of interpretation; better seek the controlled 'certainties' of history or the institution of the Church.

Let us pause for a moment over the commandment. There is a difference between the prohibition of images and the prohibition of the worship of images. The latter certainly is an activity that will quickly lead us into the realms of fantasy, and Paul describes the victims of such fantasy early in his letter to the Romans:

God has given them up to the vileness of their own desires, and the consequent degredation of their bodies, because they have bartered away the true God for a false one, and offered reverence and worship to created things instead of to the Creator who is blessed for ever; amen.

(Romans 1:24-5)

But images, both visual and literary, may act as a glass through which a vision of God may be rightly glimpsed, and as art they have the chance of being appreciated outside any superimposed controls of historical or cultural authorities. It is true that we can be taught proper 'taste' and what is aesthetically 'acceptable', but equally art and literature is always capable of slipping the noose of controls and remains essentially a creative force free from manipulation.

The last two chapters of St. Matthew's Gospel vibrate with startling imagery. The earthquakes, the saints emerging from their graves, the angel dressed in gleaming white, are all the stuff of, dare we say, a mythological literature? Here art has finely blurred the edges of event and image in an imaginative fiction which appeals in a primal way to our humanity. Such art, of course, by its very freedom from institutional control, runs the risk of rejection. But it combines a demand for hard thinking, through the resonances and associations of its images, with a passionate and even sensual quality which involves us, unlike fantasy, to the very root of our being. It is a narrative of great energy, movement and visual impact.

Suddenly there was a violent earthquake; an angel of the Lord descended from heaven; he came to the stone and rolled it away, and sat himself down on it. His face shone like lightning; his garments were white as snow. At the sight of him the guards shook with fear and lay like the dead.

(Matthew 28:2-4)

I suppose that the most obvious candidate to be called a fantasy in the New Testament is the Revelation of John. Although it stands in a tradition of apocalyptic literature, that tradition contains nothing like the form of the Christian Apocalypse. It claims to be a vision seen in a trance or dream (1:10), and it is unique in the context of the New Testament testimony to the transforming power of the Resurrection, even though there are elements of apocalyptic elsewhere in the gospels (Mark 13:3–27, Matthew 24:3–31, Luke 21:7–28).

Nevertheless I place it squarely in the category of imaginative, not fantasy, literature. For throughout the book the images are drawn from the rich inheritance of the Old Testament and recast in a new and living context, 'in Christ'. The great visions of judgement, the dragon, the wedding supper, and heaven, were deeply rooted in the Jewish imagination, absorbed into the very sense of human nature, and are now similarly etched in our own tradition with its universal language and art forms. As long as these images work upon our imagination and not upon our fancy, they remain a part of us and interpreted within our own understanding of ourselves. Only when they become fantastic and externalised do they become idolatrous and destructive, and there have certainly been perverse interpretations of Revelation which have consigned it to the realms of fantasy.

Superficially Revelation is in the form of a narrative, written as a story. I suggest that to read it as such will lead you into all sorts of difficulties. Regard it rather as a series of interrelated patterns, a finely spun web of significance in which no one image can be separated from the others. In this way you will find a whole series of harmonies being sounded at every point as the manifold references of each image are perceived. This is not to say that it can mean anything you like, but it is bound upon a multiplicity of significance which matches the complexity that we perceive in the world, in ourselves and in our experience of God.

Once again art and the literary imagination remains a

creative force essentially free from manipulation. Certainly the almost endless stream of Old Testament references need to be recognised. Perhaps, too, the sometimes allegorical references to contemporary history should be taken into our understanding and interpretation. No doubt the Babylon of 18:1–8 represents the Rome of the early Christian era. But Revelation is not simply *allegory* (see above, p. 35). In the end it remains a truly imaginative piece of literature, profoundly committed to the proclamation of the Gospel, because it is not only written for a particular audience at a particular time in history, but it challenges the imagination and the interpretative energies of everyone. Finally, we must dispense with all extraneous questions of authorship and historical origins, of structure, figurative or allegorical significance, and simply attend to the text.

> The throne of God and of the Lamb will be there, and his servants shall worship him; they shall see him face to face, and bear his name on their foreheads. There shall be no more night, nor will they need the light of lamp or sun, for the Lord God will give them light; and they shall reign for evermore.

> (Revelation 22:3–5)

This description of God's throne and its attendant worshippers indeed lies under the multiple control of a series of familiar scriptural themes and images – the clear vision of God in heaven (compare I Corinthians 13:12), light, the kingdom. But far from tying us to a pedantic unravelling of sources, the poetry of the description liberates our imaginations to reflect upon the moment of inspiration that brought them together. We have introduced a poetic method into the field of divine inspiration. We may call it divine if the imaginative fire that has been lit carries us beyond the literature and the art, beyond the author and his sources, to a sense of the presence of God in the images which have been remade in the life, death and resurrection of Jesus Christ. Whether the inspiration is of God is a question for each one of us to answer for ourselves.

In this chapter I have deliberately avoided returning to the question of historicity. It is not that I do not think that it is important, but I wanted to draw particular attention to the New Testament as *kerygma* – preaching, proclamation or testimony – as I draw near to the close of my book. The literature I have been concerned with, in so far as it is kerygmatic, is not *descriptive writing* whereby we might describe the scriptures as literally true. Its language of metaphor, symbol and myth has produced imaginative fictions which demand an imaginative response. Not in the swirling, timeless, mists of fantasy but in the profound reaches of the human imagination is the vision stretched, in hope, even where faith falls short (Mark 9:24), and the limit is laid not in the finite and actual but in the infinite and possible.

Of course, this literature does not float outside the movement of time. Its imagery and narratives look to the past in order to give meaning to the present and expectation for the future. As we have seen, the past is realised ever anew in the present, and what has already been achieved in Jesus Christ is a rebirth into a new story yet to come. The literature, and the gospel it proclaims, sustains a tension between the past and the future, between what is remembered and what is hoped for, and within this tension is preserved the Christian identity of a faith which remembers and a hope which anticipates eagerly the coming of God's kingdom. The kingdom itself, of course, is a most powerful symbol which we use repeatedly in a quasi-historical way. Indeed, the beginning and end of the history of salvation merge into parable and metaphor from the garden of Eden to the New Jerusalem. The metaphorical influence then filters into our own history, so that even within our finite concerns, eternity is at hand, glimpsed in the furnace of the imagination.

In all this, remember how critical the moment is. It is time for you to wake out of sleep, for deliverance is nearer to us now than it was when first we believed. It is far on in the night; day is near. Let us therefore throw off the deeds of darkness and put on our armour as soldiers of the light . . . Let Jesus Christ himself be the armour that you wear.

(Romans 13:11–12, 14)

8 Conclusion: The New Testament and the Literary Critic

I should not wish the word 'conclusion' to imply that I am to offer a trim and neatly packaged argument or system to enable you more effectively to resolve the problems and riddles of the New Testament. My own experience is that these writings have an endless ability to slip out of our grasp, leading us often further than we may wish to go, pointing us beyond the precisions of any organised conclusions. Yet they are not, for all that, imprecise or purely subjective.

The business of the literary critic is to try and ensure that what is a-lie does not become established as a truth. Of course, as Pontius Pilate realised, the definition of what is true is by no means easy. Nor is it made any easier when, in the first letter of John, a metaphorical description of the passage from darkness to light concludes with the claim that 'Christ has made this true, and it is true in your own experience' (2:8). This raises two questions. Is something that is true in *my* experience necessarily true in *your* experience? Also, in what sense is metaphorical language true?

Now if the business of literary criticism is truth, one may go about this business in various ways. For example, the critic may be concerned with *aesthetics* or the artistic value of literature. Or the criticism may be *descriptive*, dealing with analysis and textual meaning. Again, the critic may be primarily concerned with the relation of literature to the world and to its readers. In all this, one's sense of what is

97

true will probably stand between the 'certainties' of logical and mathematical reasoning and the 'certainties' of the experience of the senses. For my own part, in what I have said I have suggested that the literary critic may be well placed to help us respond sensitively to the language of the New Testament texts, and so by a close attention to what the evangelists and apostolic writers wrote, we may draw a little closer to the mystery which drove and inspired them. These scriptures, in part or as a whole, do not come to us as finished and resolved works of art. There is a tension between their content and their form, and the truths of which they speak are not purely of history, philosophy or literature. They point beyond all the limits which we set upon them, and our primary response must be to them as language, as structures of words which may indicate to us, without finalising, the meaning of the mysterious event of Jesus Christ.

Human beings, though children of the word, also use language for a variety of purposes, and what is used may also be abused. Certainly the way language is used in a text may be sadly misunderstood. I have argued that the New Testament writers used language, primarily though not entirely, in a metaphorical and imaginative way. We tend, I think, to regard language chiefly as a means of conveying information by attaching names to things, or as a way of organising our rational thinking. We may call these two uses *informative* and *cognitive*. But language may also be *performative*, so that we do things with words and not just talk about them. We find at the end of St. Matthew's Gospel that Jesus actually confers authority upon his disciples in a form of words:

> He said: 'Full authority in heaven and on earth has been committed to me. Go forth therefore and make all nations my disciples; baptise men everywhere in the name of the Father and the Son and the Holy Spirit, and teach them to observe all that I have commanded you.'

> (Matthew 28:18–20)

Or again, in St. Luke we find the words, 'and now I vest in you the kingship which my Father vested in me' (Luke 22:29). In the utterance of the words the deed is done.

Fourthly, language may be *expressive*, attempting to capture and convey a feeling or an experience that is elusive or even ambiguous. A paradox may best express what is most profoundly true, and the New Testament is often at its most paradoxical in its language of 'glory'.

> I beg you, then, not to lose heart over my sufferings for you; indeed, they are your glory.
>
> (Ephesians 3:13)

Words can become emotionally highly charged – one thinks in the gospels of words like 'law' and 'sabbath' – and may be powerful, even destructive, instruments.

Finally, language may be used to establish and strengthen bonds between a community of people, or between writers and readers. In the New Testament the fragments of liturgical formulae, perhaps the Lord's Prayer itself, were perhaps as familiar and well-loved in the apostolic church as the Authorized Version or the *Book of Common Prayer* are to many people today. Such *cohesive* use of language aims at one thing: 'to build up the church' (I Corinthians 14:26).

If language, therefore, can be employed in many different ways, it behoves us to be wide awake and alert to what is going on in the text in front of us. We must always be asking in what way language is being used, prepared always to respond imaginatively to its metaphors, images and symbols. Certainly we need to be intelligently aware of the background of allusion and reference, or the historicism of the text, or historical basis of its material, but never at the expense of failing to attend to the text itself. Nor should we be afraid of the sense that a work of literary art is *polysemous*, containing a variety of possible interpretations.

From the start I have worked from a notion that the New Testament makes the kerygmatic claim to be a testimony to the transforming power of the Resurrection. It uses the complex and sometimes elusive tool of language, and I see its variety partly as the result of a number of Christian communities in different circumstances voicing their growing self-awareness and attempting to explain themselves. Faith was never simple, and its 'deep truths' (I Timothy 3:9) from the start required an open and imaginative response in a variety of situations to the mystery of Jesus Christ, the child of Mary and Son of God, the promised Messiah and crucified outcast, the teacher of Galilee and Saviour of the world. The extraordinary claims of the preaching of the evangelists and apostles in the New Testament required and used, in a remarkable way, a rich assortment of the resources of language and literature. This literature is essentially written in faith. I would go so far as to say that, inasmuch as its interpretation is manifold, it has no ultimate or final meaning.

Thus, the faith of the New Testament slips through the cynicism of those who might say that, objectively, it cannot be proved or even that it is simply not true. For what is truth?

This same faith breaks down the limited and fearful vision of literalism and fundamentalism, which dare not look beyond its own blinkered conclusions and purposes. For as our knowledge now is only partial, so in our imaginations, as in the final chapters of Revelation, we may be brought to intimations of its completion, led by the metaphors of language which points beyond itself.

It is a faith which, no doubt, combines scepticism and commitment in a loving relationship which longs always to know and understand. The truth is all that we have to fear, for it will expose all falseness which is not of God (Acts 5:38–9). And yet the establishment of the truth, which is the business of the literary critic, can never make us afraid if indeed Christ is the truth (John 14:6).

We rightly say that truth leads us. For in the Gospel there is movement and no static vision. In the words of T. S. Eliot's quartet 'Little Gidding', its 'purpose is beyond the end you figured/And is altered in fulfilment'. It is perceived in time, yet timeless. The Jesus of the gospels presents us with a crisis, and in that crisis which eagerly looks forward to the establishment of God's kingly rule over all, we now live. St. Mark's Gospel is summed up in that first proclamation:

> The time has come; the kingdom of God is upon you; repent, and believe the Gospel.

> (Mark 1:15)

I have made strong claims for metaphorical language and the exercise of the imagination. I do not think that the language of the New Testament, or indeed any religious language, can be simple and unambiguous, for it deals in mysteries and with the complexity of our lives. But if it is oblique and indirect, it is not therefore imprecise. For the imagination is born of a searching intellect, and faith remains fixed upon what is most profoundly true. The language of metaphor may indeed be uncomfortable at times, for it will tend to break down the walls and structures that we have built and call reality. Yet, as we have seen, the imagination, in the metaphors and images, may be creative and disclose a greater reality which we will know to be true. For

> Divine folly is wiser than the wisdom of man, and divine weakness stronger than man's strength. My brothers, think what sort of people you are, whom God has called. Few of you are men of wisdom, by any human standard; few are powerful or highly born. Yet, to shame the wise, God has chosen what the world counts folly, and to shame what is strong, God has chosen what the world counts weakness.

> (I Corinthians 1:25–7)

I have chosen to end with this familiar passage from Paul's writings, for it serves to stress that at the heart of the New

Testament is a preaching, a *kerygma*, which first and foremost and without any initial concern to argue, defend or systematise, presents the fundamental Christian position 'in Christ' and the sheer folly of the cross. The point of the preaching was to challenge and to draw a response, and as the first disciples were sent out two by two (Mark 6:7–13, Luke 9:1–6), they were told not to instruct or explain, but to proclaim the kingdom of God and to act it out in healing and exorcism.

I believe that the continuing power of the New Testament will be revealed afresh time and again in the close attention to the literary imaginations which first gave utterance to the kerygma, no doubt first orally, and then in the written word which we have received. In diverting our minds from all secondary concerns of explanation and temporary application, such attention will recall us to the primary Christian task of preaching and proclamation, of issuing a challenge and forcing a response. It will remind us that Christian doctrine is, in principle, only an attempt to systematise the kerygma, and that a theology which cannot be preached is no theology.

My hope is to have cleared away some of the debris which so often surrounds our reading of the New Testament. No doubt I have fallen far short of my hopes. But, where language fails, it points to a silence in which the indirections of metaphor and the imperfections of symbol will be forgotten in the city where all is light and there is nothing unclean or false.

Reading List

(I have marked with an asterisk those books which I regard as most immediately helpful and illuminating.)

CHAPTER 1: ATTENDING TO THE TEXT

*Robert Alter, *The Art of Biblical Narrative* (London and Sydney: Allen & Unwin, 1981).

Paul Ricoeur, *Essays on Biblical Interpretation*, ed. Lewis S. Mudge (London: SPCK, 1981).

Joachim Rohde, *Rediscovering the Teaching of the Evangelists*, trans. Dorothea M. Barton (London: SCM, 1968).

George Steiner, *After Babel: Aspects of Language and Translation* (Oxford University Press, 1975).

David Tracy, *The Analogical Imagination. Christian Theology and the Culture of Pluralism* (London: SCM, 1981).

CHAPTER 2: THE SENSE OF HISTORY

Aristotle, Horace, Longinus, *Classical Literary Criticism*, trans. T. S. Dorsch (Harmondsworth: Penguin Books, 1965).

Dennis Nineham, *The Use and Abuse of the Bible* (London: SPCK, 1976).

M. F. Wiles, 'Does Christology rest on a mistake?', in S. W. Sykes and J. P. Clayton (eds) *Christ, Faith and History* (Cambridge University Press, 1972).

*Northrop Frye, *The Great Code. The Bible and Literature* (London, Melbourne and Henley: RKP, 1982).

J. C. Fenton, *The Gospel of St. Matthew* (Harmondsworth: Penguin Books, 1963).

*William A. Beardslee, *Literary Criticism of the New Testament* (Philadelphia: Fortress Press, 1970).

Adele Berlin, *Poetics and Interpretation of Biblical Narrative* (Sheffield: Almond Press, 1983).

Edmund Leach and D. Alan Aycock, *Structuralist Interpretations of Biblical Myth* (Cambridge University Press, 1983).

CHAPTER 3: IMAGINATION AND METAPHOR

*Terence Hawkes, *Metaphor* (London and New York: Methuen, 1972).

M. Chatterjee, *The Language of Philosophy* (The Hague, Boston, London: Nijhoff, 1981).

Dom Robert Petitpierre, *Poems of Jesus*, two volumes (London: Faith Press, 1965).

G. B. Caird, *The Revelation of St. John the Divine* (London: A. & C. Black, 1966).

Austin Farrer, *The Glass of Vision* (Westminster: Dacre Press, 1948).

Archibald MacLeish, *Poetry and Experience* (Harmondsworth: Penguin Books, 1965).

Sallie McFague, *Metaphorical Theology* (London: SCM, 1983).

*Ian T. Ramsey, *Religious Language* (London: SCM, 1957).

CHAPTER 4: THE STORY TOLD

George W. Stroup, *The Promise of Narrative Theology* (London: SCM, 1984).

David H. Kelsey, *The Uses of Scripture in Recent Theology* (London: SCM, 1975).

A. D. Nuttall, *Overheard by God* (London and New York: Methuen, 1980).

Joachim Jeremias, *The Parables of Jesus*, revised edn (London: SCM, 1963).

*Sallie McFague, *Speaking in Parables* (Philadelphia: Fortress Press, 1975).

Frank Kermode, *The Sense of an Ending* (Oxford University Press, 1967).

*Frank Kermode, *The Genesis of Secrecy* (Harvard University Press, 1979).

D. H. Lawrence, *Selected Literary Criticism*, ed. Anthony Beal (London: Heinemann, 1956).

Dan O. Via Jr, *The Parables: Their Literary and Existential Dimension* (Philadelphia: Fortress Press, 1967).

CHAPTER 5: HOLDING TO THE TRADITION

*C. H. Dodd, *The Apostolic Preaching and its Developments* (London: Hodder & Stoughton, 1963).

T. S. Eliot, 'Tradition and the Individual Talent', in *Selected Essays*, third edn (London: Faber & Faber, 1951).

A. E. Harvey (ed.) *God Incarnate: Story and Belief* (London: SPCK, 1981).

C. F. D. Moule, *The Birth of the New Testament*, second edn (London: A. & C. Black, 1966).

J. L. Houlden, *Patterns of Faith* (London: SCM, 1977).

CHAPTER 6: PROVERBIAL WISDOM

*James G. Williams, *Those Who Ponder Proverbs* (Sheffield: Almond Press, 1981).

Gerhard von Rad, *Wisdom in Israel*, trans. James D. Martin (London: SCM, 1972).

*G. B. Caird, *The Language and Imagery of the Bible* (London: Duckworth, 1980).

T. R. Henn, *The Bible as Literature* (London: Lutterworth, 1970). An expansion of 'The Bible as Literature', in Matthew Black and H. H. Rowley (eds) Peake's *Commentary on the Bible* (London: Nelson, 1962).

James L. Kugel, *The Idea of Biblical Poetry* (Yale University Press, 1981).

T. W. Manson, *The Sayings of Jesus* (London: SCM, 1961).

S. T. Coleridge, *Lay Sermons*, ed. R. J. White (Princeton University Press, 1972).

CHAPTER 7: FICTIONS AND FANTASY

*F. W. Dillistone, *The Novelist and the Passion Story* (London: Collins, 1960).

Samuel Laeuchli, *Religion and Art in Conflict* (Philadelphia: Fortress Press, 1980).

Austin Farrer, *A Rebirth of Images* (Westminster: Dacre Press, 1949).

Austin Farrer, 'Inspiration: Poetical and Divine', in *Interpretation and Belief*, ed. Charles C. Conti (London: SPCK, 1976).

John Austin Baker, *The Foolishness of God* (London: DLT, 1970).

E. S. Shaffer (ed.) *Comparative Criticism*, Volume 5 (Cambridge University Press, 1983).

Stephen Prickett, *Victorian Fantasy* (Brighton: Harvester, 1979) (Chapter 1 provides a useful description of the distinction between 'fantasy' and 'imagination').

CHAPTER 8: CONCLUSION: THE NEW TESTAMENT AND THE LITERARY CRITIC

George Watson, *The Literary Critics* (Harmondsworth: Penguin Books, 1964).

*Michael Wadsworth (ed.) *Ways of Reading the Bible* (Brighton: Harvester, 1981).

*John A. T. Robinson, *Can We Trust the New Testament?* (London and Oxford: Mowbrays, 1977).

Maurice Wiles, *Faith and the Mystery of God* (London: SCM, 1982).

Amos N. Wilder, *Early Christian Rhetoric* (London: SCM, 1964).

Amos N. Wilder, *Jesus' Parables and the War of Myths*, ed. James Breech (London: SPCK, 1982).

Sir Edwyn Hoskyns and Noel Davey, *The Riddle of the New Testament* (London: Faber & Faber, 1931).

List of Scriptural Passages

Index